MW01595723

DEDICATION

"To be a star, you must shine your own light, follow your own path, and don't worry about the darkness, for that is when the stars shine brightest"

To my Guardian Angel Paul, who might or might not have been my Paternal Grandfather. Thank you for the inspirations, the prodding and the love. This is your book!

"There's room for everybody on the planet to be creative and conscious if you are your own person. If you're trying to be like somebody else, then there is isn't."
Tori Amos

CONTENTS

I wonder if I've been changed in the night? Let me think. Was I the same when I got up this morning? I almost think I can remember feeling a little different. But if I'm not the same, the next question is 'Who in the world am I?' Ah, that's the great puzzle!
Alice in Wonderland

ACKNOWLEDGMENTS

Writing a book is not something one should do without a tribe to support him. I've been fortunate to accumulate a group of lovely and helpful people who have been able to help me bring Middle Aged Crazy to life through their encouragement, their stories and their advice.

Teresa, and my kids Suzanne, Elizabeth, Rachel and James have been a source of support and inspiration. Thank you all for allowing me to become Me.

The concept of becoming an artist in mid life was inspired by the life work of Dr. Wayne Dyer and by author Seth Godin. Authors Daniel Pink and Ken Robinson have also been huge influences on developing the theories of Middle Aged Crazy.

My writing team includes professional speaker Charlyn Shelton, an accomplished writer and someone who has read every word I've ever written while offering love, guidance and common sense. The amazingly talented Betsy Streeter, illustrator and muse was the first person the angels told me to call and they were right. She has been an angel herself. Thom Scott has offered occasional brilliance when I have needed it most.

I've written much of this work through my blog and received such valuable feedback from the Middle Aged Crazies who hang out on my web page. They have helped to shape this book more than they will ever know. Lisa, Theresa, Candy, Mel, Donna, Melissa and a host of other talented people have served as sounding boards and muses.

Thank you from the bottom of my heart. Rick

Come Play!
Middle Aged Crazy is a community of people who have joined together to share work, feelings and laughter. I hope you'll come meet us on Facebook or on my Blog.

http://www.facebook.com/pages/
Middle-Aged-Crazy-Because-
Being-Creative-Can-Save-Your-
Life/108008349221794

www.middleagedcrazy.com

1 Who Defines You?

Ray's Story: "I swear to God, another one of these sales meetings and I am going to burst into flames in front of my staff. What happened? I was going to make a difference, going to change the world, I was going to be this great writer. Now I'm wearing a suit and wing tips. Wing tips! Don't tell me that the entire reason for my existence was to sell stuff to impulse buyers. Is that what will be on my tombstone, "He sold a lot of stuff?" When do I get to be me?"

Lynn's Story: "Yes Rachel, I am your Mother. No, I am not stupid. I understand that all of your friends are going and yes, believe it or not, I still don't want you to go to the rock concert. You are only 13. Yes; I have been to rock concerts, does the name Woodstock mean anything to you?"
"I have raised her, and her sisters, while working at the bank for twenty years. What happened? I was going to paint, I was going to be this artist. Now I am my Mother. That's a joke, My Mother! I love my kids, I am proud that I have been a great single parent. But I was going to change the way people look at the world. When do I get to be me?

Chances are, you pride yourself on being unselfish, on living your life in the service of others... I get that. But, isn't there a fine line between being someone who serves others and a spectator? It's easy, in our culture to forget to make time for ourselves, to live our own life. With all we do for others, it's easy to forget to be "me"

How much of your life do you spend watching other people do things? There are a lot of issues that accompany this, "when do I get to be me?" question, aren't there? We have obligations, we've made decisions that require our attention, money is always an issue. We end up being slaves, not in the literal definition of the word, but slaves none the less. We become slaves to our jobs, our bills, and our obligations, until, pretty soon, we feel like we are watching our very lives go by.

We watch our spouse, our kids, our boss, our clients... When did we decide it was ok to be a spectator to this life we've been given? Do you feel like you even had a choice? Have circumstances just taken over? Do you feel like you lost control of your own destiny?

I know, you are busy, but how much of what you do is *for* you? Oh, we are busy, I know, I am too! We put miles on the car, in airports and waiting in front of soccer fields. We spend time taking care of everyone else, it seems like we don't have a moment to ourselves (or for ourselves). In between commutes, meetings, soccer practice and grocery shopping, when are we supposed to write that book? When are we supposed to put all of our great, creative ideas to use?

We watch sports on TV, watch movies, watch American Idol... We read People Magazine, we watch Oprah, we follow Celebrity Gossip... How many things do you "watch" instead of "do"? Do you lean forward or lean back when you get to sit down at night? Yes, we are so exhausted that we often collapse in front of the TV. We long to be entertained. A little celebrity gossip, a good ballgame, a story; anything to quiet the mind, to help us regenerate, to help us cope. Sometimes, we medicate, because life seems to be just a little beyond our grasp, we want to slow it down.

We have become a nation of spectators. We like to be entertained... If it isn't television, it's the internet or maybe, if the stars are aligned, a really good book. (Thanks for taking the time to read this one.)

Did you ever wonder, when do I get to quit supporting, watching and worrying about other people and when do I get to be me? It's not selfish to want to do something that you want to do: it's natural. Only, we seem to have forgotten how.

I am convinced that we all came to this earth for a reason and that reason, as buried as it might be, can be found by rediscovering our creative side, by becoming, in our own quiet way, an artist. Wayne Dyer says,

"Find your passion. Your passion is what stirs your soul and makes you feel like you're totally in harmony with why you showed up here in the first place."

Creativity is not talent. Talent helps, but it isn't required to find something inside of you. And: that's what finding your own creativity is about, reaching deep into your soul, when you create, you reconnect with your source. For now, at least, suspend the notion that you have to create something that someone else approves of.

You don't.

"Oh she is so talented!" Might be a nice thing to hear, but it is totally irrelevant. You don't have to write something a publisher will accept, paint something a gallery will sell, sing a song Nashville will buy or dance like you are going to win a reality show.

Nope. All you have to do is to begin to think like an artist.

Why? Well, I'll tell you more about this later, but, for now, let's just say because it is cool. My suggestion: add "Create cool stuff" to your To Do List everyday; your whole day will be better. You'll spend the time before you create looking forward to creating, you'll be engaged while you create, and you'll feel good about your creation when you are finished. When you close your eyes at night, you'll realize you spent the whole day thinking like an artist, and that's a magnificent feeling.

This book is designed to give you permission to take care of you. I'm going to help you give yourself permission to listen to your soul, to find a new way to make it happy. I'm going to ask you to begin to look at life through the eyes of an artist, even if you don't believe you have an artistic bone in your body. I want you to understand that you are a creation and a creator, you are creating a life everyday.

Here's a little secret: I am not going to teach you anything: I can't. I can only SHOW you things, you have to teach yourself. You know what you came here for, it's time to listen to your heart. They say, when the student is ready, the teacher will appear.

Here's what I will do: I will lay out the tools you'll need to begin the journey. That's a lot. I've spent my lifetime preparing to tell you the stuff I'm going to share. From a career in business to a new life as an author, I have lived Middle Aged Crazy. My research has led me to find out what happens to us in middle age and why creativity is crucial to saving you. I've learned about education and why it is not serving us (or our children) when it comes to finding fulfillment.

I've found out why we forget our dreams, why we feel ashamed to follow them, why fear can stop us. I've read everything I could find about source, where does inspiration come from?

Mostly, I've talked to a lot of you. The magic of social media has made research phenomenally easy, I've literally talked to thousands of people going through middle age, who have wondered: "When do I get to be me?" It's been quite an education!

Many of them came to this question as empty nesters. They spent a lifetime taking care of their kids until one day they drove them to campus and drove home alone. Now what? No more Little League, no more recitals, no preparing dinners for a tribe. Wow, what's left?

Relationships, there's a big one. How many of us came home from that campus to an empty house, or to a spouse who didn't understand us? I've talked to a lot of people who need an outlet to express their frustration, their sadness, their emptiness, their rage. Living in an abusive or empty relationship is tragedy and those who feel powerless often find their power through creativity.

Emptiness, loneliness, wondering if we have wasted a lot of time are all part of this middle aged thing. We've had a lifetime of making decisions and now, no matter who we are, we begin to wonder if making decisions the same way will serve us in the rest of our lives. It's a natural thing to wonder if we are to remain on the course we embarked upon or it time to head for a new destination.

What age is middle age? It isn't a number, obviously, if we knew the date of our death we could simply divide by 2! No, middle age is when we have a glimpse at mortality and begin to wonder, what will my legacy be? How will people remember me? Will I leave this world a better place? What can I do to feel happy and proud about the life I have lived?

When you look at mid-life in this context, it isn't a bad place to spend some time. You have wisdom, some stories to tell, you can see a bigger picture. A lot of you have embraced mid-life, instead of getting caught in it like a trap, you have welcomed reaching a point where you can make some positive choices. I'm not a big fan of that whole "Mid-Life crisis" thing; life happens and crisis come along. It's too easy to blame them on age.

The economy has brought many of you here. Let's face it, if your job can be outsourced to Asia or done by a robot, your life has changed. Welcoming creativity, for you, is a survival skill. Robots, it turns out, aren't very creative! Seeing the world with new eyes, finding answers to questions no one has seen before and calling yourself an artist is not a bad idea. When we catch the rare artist who grasps business concepts, we call him something else: We call him a visionary, a genius or an entrepreneur.

One of my favorite authors, Seth Godin, is one of the world's most revered experts on marketing, innovation and competitiveness, his message: it takes artists to succeed in business today. Reading from a manual, sticking to the playbook won't get it done anymore, it takes artists, people who bring passion and creativity to their work to be successful in business today. Businesses are built by artists and killed by legal departments. Find me a company run by it's former corporate attorney and I'll short it.

There is pain on this road, we know that. In talking with you I have been surprised by how much pain there is. I wasn't ready for all the loneliness, the pain and the love. What started out as a journey to get people to plug into their artistic side has turned into a rescue mission. Who gets rescued? So far: Me. Why does creativity save your life? Because when you bury it, you bury a lot of stuff with it, like emotions.

Blanking out in front of the TV every night is a cheap narcotic. The lovely people I've met in creating this Middle Aged Crazy community are my mirrors, I realize I am not alone on this path. None of us are broken, we don't need to be fixed, yet we realize something is missing. Our Creative Beast wants to come out, our soul wants to be happy, not numbed.

Ignoring your creative side, I think, is a sign that we are ignoring something bigger, like life. Does picking up a few drawing pencils change everything? Not exactly. Picking up a few drawing pencils and beginning to look at life as an artist: now that does change everything. Finding the humor, beauty, joy and pain in every situation is what artists do. Artists are more sensual, more observant, more engaged in their own life. Isn't being engaged what it's all about?

Why? Because, the best way to create is to tap into emotion; emotion raises you from technician to artist. Only, this little tapping into emotion thing is irreversible; empathy, pain and deeper feelings in general come with the process and aren't turned off easily. (Speaking of process, not all artists fit into any one category, all of our processes and emotions are individualized, we've had a lifetime to develop this stuff.) The benefit of having a community like M.A.C. is that you realize you are not alone, there are other people out here who are on the same journey and that makes all the difference.

Our cadre of artists, from all creative disciplines, is on my website (www.middleagedcrazy) to support you, to teach you, to share your journey. We can talk about how resistance gets us, how other people don't. We can wonder together how to channel all of our creative ideas, how to deal with some of the pain that comes with reaching mid life. Most of all, we can talk about what hurts and how we fill that hole with creation.

Know that wanting to improve your life does not mean that something is broken or that you need to be fixed. Know that you have experiences and stories that no one else has and, once you find that right medium to share them, life gets better. It has for me, letting my Creative Beast out has made all the difference.

The first time I was introduced somewhere as an author, I looked around the room to see if someone would yell "Fraud!" I worried the Pulitzer Police would be hot on my trail, "Business Guy Convicted of Impersonating Writer" was the headline I imagined. Then, I took a breath, always a good plan. I surveyed the room and realized I was the only guy there with a book on Amazon, the only person there who had a relationship with thousands of readers. Son of a gun: I was an author.

Who gets to define you if not you? Suppose you started introducing yourself as a painter, as a musician, as an actor? Would anyone check? Wouldn't most people just assume you were telling the truth? What is the truth anyway? (If you write, you are a writer. If you wait tables in L.A. you are an actor) I think it would be really positive if we identified ourselves by our passions and not what we do to make a living.

This is especially easy for creative people, most artists, when you think about it, have "day jobs". The day the actor stops thinking of himself as an actor and identifies himself as a waiter is probably the first day he contemplates suicide.

When I used to travel, it was dressed as the Wall Street guy I was. Briefcase, power tie, wingtips... And it sucked. No one talked to you, people called you sir, they assumed you were a rich Republican... You even played the role, I'd carry a Wall Street Journal for God's sake! Ever try to read that thing?

Then, one day, I took a chance. I was flying to Las Vegas from Orlando for a speech. I wore jeans, cowboy boots and a tee shirt to the airport for a cross country flight. For good measure I threw a guitar case on my back. Oh My God! On the tram to the gate another musician, headed to Nashville, asked me where I was playing ("Vegas"). Hot women checked me out ("Is that Glen Frey, isn't he in the Eagles? Like Glenn Frey would fly commercial on Airtran!). Other business guys looked at me in envy. The quality of conversation went up a thousand degrees on the interesting scale. I was the real me, for a change. At least I was a different me, one I really wanted to be.

I was having a little bit of a masquerade party, no different than the guys who wear Harley gear and pretend to be bikers. No different than the guys who wear Nike shirts and golf shoes to follow Tiger Woods around at a tournament. I redesigned myself, only, in this design, I was playing the real me, as told by my Creative Beast.

Was I lying about anything? No, I never claimed to be a professional musician, in fact, I didn't claim to be anything. I do, in fact, play the guitar, (certainly not professionally) I am passionate about the semi-in-tune notes that come from my strings. After my trip, I began to think of myself as real guitar player. I think my playing even got better!

If you bowl in a league, you are a bowler. If you play golf, you are a golfer. So, why is it different for artists? We are, after all, creations ourselves and, in turn, we create. If you are truly passionate about your creative outlet, wear it with pride. "Yes, I am a brain surgeon during the week, but I play in a rock and roll band on the weekends!" "I am a painter, yes, I am also raising three children!" "yes, I write a blog, I'm a banker during the day."

Like I said, you get to define you, you are creating your life. Who says your boss gets your soul too? A few of us have jobs that match our passion and we are blessed. Some of us, if we brought more passion to our jobs, would be happier and more fulfilled. Some of us have to redefine the role that our job has in our life, we need to begin to look at it as a means to an end: the way we support our creative habit.

My hope is that this book helps you to have the confidence to begin to think of yourself as an artist. You don't have to abandon your obligations and commitments to do so. Re-discovering your creative side is an invitation to lead a happier, more fulfilling life. It is an invitation to tell your stories, to feel real emotion again, to, perhaps, change the world.

When do you get to be you? I hope it is today. I hope today is the day you start listening to your soul, I hope today is the day you decide it is ok to take care of you, I hope today is the day you make something cool.

Something wonderful happens when you live as an artist. Writers hear words differently, painters see everything as potential scenes, dancers begin to hear music in the wind. Artist are more sensuous, more observant, more alive. That beats watching sitcoms and passing out on the couch every time.

Every time.

Listen, the noise you hear is your Creative Beast. He wants to come out and play. A word of warning, if you don't let him out, he will tunnel out, and that's not a good thing!

Chapter One Exercises:

1.) First off: You are not broken. There is nothing wrong with wanting to experience life as a full participant. Somewhere along the way; many of us decided that we would live to serve others. That's great, but remember, You Matter. Are you a spectator? How much of your life is spent watching other people do things? Creation requires participation. This is going to be hard, but for one week, I invite you to write down how much time you spend watching TV, watching other people, and here's the tougher thing: supporting other people. You know: watching your kids, helping your boss, doing something for your spouse. If you are like a lot of people I talk to, even though you are very busy, most of your waking hours are spent watching and supporting others' activities.

While actively loving someone else through action is AWESOME, When do you get to be you? This week, you are going to find out how much time you have. I suggest a yellow legal pad and a week full of writing down EVERYTHING you do for JUST YOU:

Most of us will fall into one of two categories:

A. We have been watching a lot more TV than we realized and we actually have tons of free time. Start Creating!!!

B. We are so busy taking care of everyone else that we don't have time to be ourselves. Do you hear that? Yes, it's the rattling cage of your Creative Beast.

2.) Time for an artist's mission statement, remember when I asked you what your reason for being here is? Well:

Why Am I Here on Earth and what can I do to better demonstrate that mission?

What would I like to Create (and why)

C. What Creative Pursuit Gets You the Most Excited?

But then, shall I never get any older than I am now? That'll be a comfort, one way -- never to be an old woman -- but then -- always to have lessons to learn!
Alice in Wonderland

2 Remembering You

Ray's story: I don't mean to whine. I've made my choices along the way and I have a good life. Big screen TV's, the Mercedes, the nice vacations... It's just that sometimes; something is missing. I feel like I am being called to do something more, that my talent has been diverted. If I went home and declared myself to be a writer, my wife would freak out, my kids would laugh, my company would get very nervous. But, I can write, I don't know if I could write a bestseller, but I think I have something to say. I've always chased the money, the promotion, the next customer. I'm not getting any younger, when do I get to do something just for me?

Lynn's story: I've made some choices in life that I don't regret, exactly, but they sure limited my options. Of course I am glad I had my baby, even if I was in high school when she came along. I've been in survival mode ever since! I've reached a point where survival isn't good enough anymore. I matter. I've been to the seminars, I've read all the self help books, I'm ready to make an impact on the world, at least beyond this apartment and the bank. I think I have something to say! I am more than someone who can drive kids around and open checking accounts. I've loved art since I was a kid, I haven't done anything about it... except, once in a while, I like to sketch a little at work. I feel like art is calling me now, I have something to say. So what if it is silly or costs a little money. Why can't I do this for me?

It's a pretty radical thing to want to be YOU. You are a Mom, a Dad, an employer, an employee. You play roles, you live behind a mask. Do you even remember who "YOU" is?

To some people, the very mention of the word "Self" is an anathema. The word conjures visions of yuppies in a circle and chanting "Me, Me, ME! Taking care of me is seen to be the supreme act of selfishness. The backlash to the self help industry is understandable, certain people have taken the self esteem thing a bit too far. When someone starts to talk in psycho babble and appears to become very "selfish", it can be disconcerting to watch them go through radical changes.

Where I live, on the East Coast, we say they are very "California". In a culture where people don't attend seminars or read self help books, those that do are looked at like hippies at a GOP convention. You get sort of a patient smile and nod from them, as if you need to go back on your meds.

"Weren't you worried about being you when you had those kids?" "When you married her?" "When you quit college?" "When you took out that mortgage?" "Wasn't that you?"

Yes, we have made decisions with all the best intentions, with all the information we had at our disposal. Nobody makes bad decisions on purpose. That doesn't mean you can't decide to grow. Deciding to make some changes certainly doesn't invalidate all of your past decisions and assumed obligations.

This book is NOT about walking away from your life.

It is about making your life better.

The experiences, relationships and obligations that you have should not be ignored. By our middle years, we begin to look back on a life of decision making and wonder if those decisions need a little revision for the rest of our lives. Sometimes, we get so caught up in the roles that we've assumed, that we are afraid there is no deviation, that we can't get to be ourselves, that we can't do what it takes to make our soul happy.

Making your soul happy is not a selfish choice, it is the most healthy choice a human being can make. Deciding to release your creative side is a choice you make out of love, not anger or fear. Most of the time, decisions that come from love result in a positive outcome. When you make decisions for you highest and best good, you are choosing a path with richer experiences, deeper relationships and more satisfaction.

My research has show that we are often afraid to be ourselves, afraid to realize our dreams. Why? Because we make a lot of decisions and choices based on expediency, on convenience and on the short term. When we begin to talk with our soul, we are going past the superficial, going to a level that can be uncomfortable and even scary. When you wonder, "What is my reason for being here?" you are getting to a philosophical plane that many of us will do anything to avoid.

Congratulations, if you have come this far, you are a seeker, a pioneer! So, what is all this "Make your soul happy" stuff? Why are you here?

You can call this feeling a lot of thing: your "meaning", your calling, your "Damon", "your reason for being", your mission, my genius, the will of God...

I just like to think I'm making my soul happy.

I don't want to get anymore religious, spiritual or creationist here than you want me to, when you start talking about these things you can make people squirm. All I can tell you is what I believe. I believe that we are all creations and creators. I believe we are designed in the image of our creator and that we have a need to create something ourselves. We do it, every day, we create a life, our own life. But, is that life that we are creating the one we came here to build? If we don't take responsibility for this life we are building, who will?

"Rick, is this a self help book or a book about creativity?" Yes. It is about finding yourself through creativity. It's about Releasing Your Creative Beast, that little monster who wants to help you live a more imaginative and creative life. My premise is quite simple, if you release your beast, your life will improve. It will improve at work and at home. You will look at the world differently, you will use your emotions differently, you will solve more problems, including personal ones. In short, life will be fun again.

As I said, we don't always feel right about making our soul happy. Paulo Coelho, author of the classic book, The Alchemist, gives us 4 reasons that we fail to pursue our dream. The Alchemist is a fable about making your life better and it has positively affected millions of lives all over the world.

The success of the Alchemist caught everyone by surprise, including the humble Coehlo. He released his creative beast and the world discovered and then loved his work. In the tenth anniversary addition of the book, he reflected on the Alchemist's impact and the lessons he's learned from it, including these very relevant reasons that we don't pursue our dreams.

1. "Our personal calling is so deeply buried that we have forgotten it." We get busy, we take care of others, we worry about paying the bills, getting ahead, surviving, we forget about all the things that we used to plan to do "some day."

There's a phrase we hear and eventually start to use: "That would be nice, but let's be realistic." We have careers, kids, Cub Scout Meetings, Little League and before you know, that "I'm going to learn to play guitar someday" promise you made to yourself is forgotten. "Sure it would be nice to play guitar, it would be nice to do a lot of things," we think to ourselves. "Let's get real, when do I have time for all that extra stuff?"

What's the difference between an actual calling and one of those extra things you might get around to someday? The calling won't go away, that's what. Your Creative Beast is tenacious, he will keep reminding you of your calling until you pay attention. I suggest that ignoring him is done at your own peril!

Ignoring him leads to illness, to bad relationships, to grumpiness. If you are meant to write, someday, you will have to write. You won't worry about all the practical questions like "Who will buy my book", you'll just start to write. You'll be better for it. That calling is in there somewhere, even if you've forgotten it.

2. LOVE. Surprising isn't it? Love is the most powerful force in the world and creation is its best by product. It's ironic that love can also keep us from creating. We are afraid of hurting those around us and abandoning everything to get what we want. Many of us would rather give up our own dreams to take care of those we love. But, funny thing, our dreams have a way of staying with us. Is that why you are here? Is something calling you?

Like I said, your calling is your calling, you can deny it all you want, but it won't go away. The parent who gives up on her dream is not doing the child any favors. Like I said, picking up a paintbrush or a violin doesn't mean you are abandoning anybody, yet millions of us give up on our dream every day, for the sake of others.

"Rick isn't that a bit extreme?" No, being selfless is one thing but you weren't put on this earth to ignore your own calling. Many really busy people are really busy out of choice. Many have lost control of their own schedule. Running your kids all over town or working until midnight is noble but so is taking a little time to be you.

You need to ask, are you coming from a place of love or fear on this one? Is your reluctance to find your creative voice actually fear masked as concern for others? A Course in Miracles says, "When others speak from fear, anger or pain, they are really just saying I want to be safe and loved." Sometimes, your wanting to love and be loved can keep you from stretching, from taking chances. I'll talk more in Chapter 3 about this one.

3. Fear of Failure: Once we remember our life's purpose and decide to pursue our dream, the next roadblock is a white knuckled fear of failure. What if we make all the required changes to chase our dreams and then fail? What is left? Is it better to have our dream as an ideal, to exist on a special place we call "Someday Isle" than it is to try to succeed and fail miserably? "Yea, someday I'll write a book" is a lot easier on you than, "I wrote my book and got 59 rejection letters."

We don't talk about fear as adults, at least not every day. We have the answers, we power on; we are invincible. At least we are expected to be, vulnerability is weakness.

When it comes to creation, we are delving into the unknown, fear is part of the trip! If you aren't stretching, you aren't growing, so I invite you to embrace the fear, to expect it and be ready to learn from it.

4. The final and most dangerous fear is that of realizing our dream. Yes, if we have spent our life denying ourselves happiness and self fulfillment, we can sabotage ourselves when on the verge of success. Deep down, we don't feel worthy of success, we are afraid to become the butterfly who emerges from the cocoon. Success means we have grown, we have changed.

Our evil foe in all things creative is a horrible creature known as Resistance. He knows our weak spots and how to prevent us from being successful. We'll talk a lot about overcoming resistance later in the book, but know this: self sabotage is subtle and deadly. It can strike by a simple decision to set your work aside and never pick it up again. It can be you listening to someone's tone of voice and mistakenly deciding they hate your work, whatever the reason, our subconscious can work against us.

You can over come these obstacles, I have. Once you decide to move forward, to get off the bench and get in the game, you can play BIG. If your dream, your purpose has gotten so lost that you have forgotten it, don't despair, it will come back to you. If you look for it.

I suggest you reintroduce yourself to your soul: get quiet, meditate, pray. Try to remember what you loved to do when you were a child, what were your dreams? What are your dreams? What would you like to create? Why? What do you love to do? What would make your soul happy?

If you don't love the concept of throwing away everything in your life, don't worry: you don't have to. You can make changes but it will go easier if you announce your attentions to those around you. Will your friends and family support you if you explain to them what you'd like to do? Can you begin to fulfill your dream if you got help with your schedule? Maybe you don't have to give everything up to grow.

If you have to make major life changes, are you doing so out of love? If you are moving forward out of love, your family will know. Ultimately, it is your life, you know you haven't signed your hopes and dreams away. And; how are you at asking for help? It might be time to get better at it. If you been waiting for your kids and spouse to read your mind, you'll be waiting a long time. (As a parent and spouse, I can tell you subtlety is wasted on me, speak up!)

Are you hung up on that failure/ excellence thing? Here's the thing about failure: You will fail. I'd like to tell you that you won't but failure is part of the journey. If you don't fail and fairly often, you are not stretching far enough. Will you learn from it and move on? Will you grow from failure? I think you will. Get off your own back and remember this ancient Gregorian Chant taught to me by Chicken Soup for the Soul creator Jack Canfield. Jack says, when faced with fear that paralyzes you, recite this:

"Aw what the heck, go for it anyway."

Are you a self saboteur? If you convince yourself that you are worthy, that you deserve to be engaged in life, to be fulfilled, to make your soul happy, you will not sabotage your success, you will welcome it. You will power through resistance like an army of angels, creation trumps resistance. Every time.

I believe in you, do you believe in you? Have you employed Grace? It seems impossible to talk about creating something without bringing a spiritual component into the discussion. I've already stated my case that creation is divine. No matter how you define divinity, there is something about making something new that connects you to a power bigger than yourself. The ego can only take you so far, artists are quick to admit that their gift is unexplainable, it comes from somewhere beyond themselves. Why does creativity save your life? Because creation IS life.

A look at the headlines tells us we live in a graceless age. I wanted to talk about something called Grace, at least as I understand it. In a time where you have to be very careful using church words, least you offend the agnostic or the fervent, I can't help but think about Grace. It defines my life. Grace has changed the way I look at the world, the way I live, the way I think.

Grace makes creation effortless, it's when your angels type through your hands, it's when just the right words come out at just the right time. Grace is the feeling I get on the water, when I am surrounded by dolphins and immersed in nature. It's that all too rare feeling that we are connected to all life, that we are all one. Grace is a Mother's forgiveness, a child's first giggle, a stranger who holds a door for you, it's someone who knows what you mean even if you say it all wrong. Grace is answered prayers, it's the love of your life.

Grace lasts longer than happiness, it trumps anger, it overcomes loneliness. Grace is not a temporary feeling, more than any single emotion; it is a state of being. Grace enhances emotion, it makes life better, it trumps the self. Grace is your soul mate, it's your muse, it is your life preserver.

Throughout history the smartest minds have argued whether grace is given or earned. I'm not bright enough to join this debate, except to say, I have done almost nothing to earn grace yet it flows to me in an endless river. I'm certain that those who try to parcel out Grace or who tell me I am not earning my share are defining Grace differently than I am. I know when Grace is there, I know I will have a better day if I remember to look for it, I know that my bad days are the days when I forgot to look.

We say people "walk with grace" and that isn't a religious term. We admire people who handle problems with Grace, we say Grace before Thanksgiving dinner, sadly, some people fall from Grace. Grace is an acknowledgment that we are more than animals, that we know how to handle adversity, that we know how to find our higher self. I'm old enough to remember when we said someone was "classy" (not in a Vegas lounge act kind of way), it meant they had Grace. People with Grace light up a room, they attract more light, they channel from a higher place.

Jealousy, possessiveness, ego, anger and hatred are the enemies of grace, yet grace can easily trounce them. Artists who remember to tune into grace hear more notes, paint with more color, they find their work going beyond ego and into the hearts of their audience. (They call it Soul Music for a reason.) When we harden our hearts, grace penetrates the wall.

Grace is the greatest of love and those of us who have lost it are doomed to spend our lives trying to forget it while, at the same time, searching madly for it again.

I hope that you find Grace when you begin to create. I hope that you find that special time when you are not quite sure what is going to come out next and let it come out anyway, when you learn to "trust the feeling". Because when you do that you are touching the supernatural, if only for a few seconds.

Artists call that feeling "Flow" and when you are there, time flies and stands still at once, you are drawing from something wonderful, something unlimited. Flow is like finding the groove in music, it's a place you go. Once you've been there, been in Flow, you are hooked, "the first one is free".

Before you say, I'm not that talented, I'm not worthy, I could never get there, just stop. You have experienced Flow. There's a song that you have to play over and over, there's something you've read that you can't put down, there was something... somewhere, that totally captivated your soul. It might have been making love, maybe it was in church, it was the trip of a lifetime. You have already experienced flow. Wouldn't you like to go back there again?

That's how you find you, that's how you make your soul happy, you find this mysterious flow, you find this peculiar combination of concentration and ecstasy and you go with it. And when you do, you are living like an artist.

Artists create, they have spirit, they are "enthusiastic". They are plugged into source. And I don't care if you are selling Avon products or managing a factory, if you come at life from the viewpoint of an artist, your days will be fuller, you will be engaged in the world around you.

That's not such a bad way to spend your day.

Chapter 2 Exercises

A.) You are a creation, you are a creator. It might be a good idea to write down how you perceive your source of creativity. I'd like you to reflect on inspiration and creation and write down what that's like for you, can you describe Flow?

B.) According to Paul Coleho, author of the Alchemist, we have a dream when we are young, but, for various reasons, we stop chasing it. For each of Paul's reasons, below, jot down some notes about times you have set your dream aside.

1.   We forget our dream. What WAS your dream and how did you forget it?

2.   We often quit chasing our dream because of our love for others. Have you done so? If so, how?

3.   Fear of Failure can paralyze us. What fears are keeping you from moving forward to attain your dream?

4.   Self Sabotage becomes an issue when we are close to achieving our goal. Resistance, our evil foe, tends to grab us right when we are within reach of the prize. Now's the time to get it out, how do you set yourself up for failure?

C.) Time for a meeting (or two). Before you tell your spouse, family or co-workers why you need more time to become this artist person, it might be a good idea to practice by writing down what you are going to tell them. Remember, come from a place of love!

All my life I had been looking for something, and everywhere I turned someone tried to tell me what it was. I accepted their answers too, though they were often in contradiction and even self-contradictory. I was naïve. I was looking for myself and asking everyone except myself questions which I, and only I, could answer. It took me a long time and much painful boomeranging of my expectations to achieve a realization everyone else appears to have been born with: that I am nobody but myself. ~Ralph Ellison, "Battle Royal"

3 Why Art?
(Or: You Can't Make Me Draw!)

Ray's Story: "It's kind of hard to imagine myself as an artist; I mean I get it: writers are artists too, but I can't draw, can't sing, can't paint. I'll tell you what, I started playing a little guitar and every once in a while, I feel like I am really expressing myself when I play. I'm expressing feelings and I was afraid I'd shut them down all together! I'm getting better at that when I write too, I'm able to express myself better. I've noticed it even helps me at work, to bring a little more imagination to the job! It's more fun to be me now!"

Lynn's Story: "I said "I am an artist", but really, what was I doing? I wasn't creating any art, I was just thinking about creating art. The best thing I ever did was take that art class, I'm actually doing something now, and, you know what? I have a little talent! I think about what I'm going to paint all day, I paint in the evening, before bed, and then I dream about what I painted all night. It's a lot more fun to be me now!"

Even if you don't believe you have an artistic bone in your body, focusing on creation is an important part of rediscovering your passion for life. That creation can be anything from keeping a journal (or blog), to learning a new creative skill like painting or dancing. The world is crying for creativity and if you simply begin to approach your current roles in life from a more creative and artistic perspective, you will be a more effective, and happier person.

So, why art? What if you're like me and can't draw, don't want to paint or don't want to ever, ever venture into a Hobby Lobby? Certainly, I am NOT saying that if you buy a paint by number set, start to draw on the back of envelopes or take a dance class that all of your problems will go away. Artists have their share of problems too.

I'm really talking about releasing your inner artist, I'm talking about creativity. Computers and outsourcing have taken care of a lot of the jobs that paid people with good memories, it's important, in today's world to approach life more like an artist and less like a computer chip.

Creativity is defined as applied imagination. Let's talk about that for a minute: imagination is great, everyone has one, some of us have more active imaginations than others... It's the "applied" part that is a little more of a challenge, as the writer Seth Godin says, "Artists Ship." Creativity implies creation, actually "creating" something. By focusing on inspiration, by listening to your Creative Beast, you will find that everything in life is just a little different than it used to be. Here's what I wrote a little while ago about art and creation:

"I talk about "Soul" a lot. I'm not trying to convert you, not trying to recruit you to my religious sect. Motown music is Soul Music, it comes from deep down, from within. Our soul is our inner being, our subconscious, the voice we hear inside of our brain. I believe that your soul is the real you, the spirit that animates your human body. Soul is also called "Life Force". (Use the force Luke = I'm a Soul Man)

So many words that relate to creativity lead us back to soul. You are said to be inspired when you come up with a good idea, artists are called creators, what a coincidence: God is known as a creator and the source of inspiration.

If you have an "inspiration" you get enthusiastic, and that's a word whose Greek origins means, "The God Within." Artists are also called originators and producers, they are considered to be inventive and innovative.

Life itself is referred to as existence, being and spirit. A friend of mine calls creative people "passionate people". We passionate people are filled with spirit, which is also a name for God. God told Moses, "I am". It's not too much of a stretch, to say that God is Life and Life is Creation. (And if you don't believe in God, that's ok, this can be viewed as a good linguistic exercise).

We reach a point in life, some earlier, some later, where we look for meaning. Meaning is worth, significance, substance and intention. That's our soul, our spirit, asking those questions. The body can be happy with cheeseburgers, beer and naps. It is the spirit within that asks us to find out why we exist.
It all connects! You are an artist!"

We came here as creations, from creation. As Wayne Dyer said, if you take a glass of water from the ocean, it is still water. Spill it on the beach and it will eventually return to source. Finding our own inspiration, our inner artist, is licensing our spirit to reconnect to source. If you can get an artist to tell you where his creation comes from, he'll often tell you it comes from somewhere outside of him, he just channels it. It comes from source.

God is also called Love. Releasing your creativity is an act of love, a spiritual act. When you connect with creativity, you are drawing on the super natural.

Namaste."

That's why I talk about Releasing Your Creative Beast. If you pay attention, if you listen, there is no shortage of inspiration out there, how much of it, you might wonder, do you ignore everyday because you haven't been thinking of yourself as an artist? I believe that if you don't pay attention to your creative urges, you are playing with fire. If you don't let your creative beast out, he will tunnel out. (And that's not always a good thing.)

The Beast is the messenger from your soul to the real world. By giving voice to your creative urges, to find a way to tell YOUR story, you proclaim your uniqueness and you share your gift. By mid life, we have unique experiences, different points of view, we relate to the world differently. You have taken a blank canvas called life and created something on it. A masterpiece? I think so. You are you, there is no one else who sees life through your eyes, there is not another you. That's a masterpiece.

If you and I went on a trip together, if we went on a trip to say, Italy and came home to write about it, we would probably tell completely different stories. No ONE can write YOUR book. I might notice the beautiful scenery, you might notice the art. You might be enamored by the food, I might discover the glories of chianti. We all see the world through our own lens that is shaped by experience, beliefs and perceptions. It is time to bring your personal flavor to the world... Piacheri!

You are a creation. You create. You are an artist. It doesn't matter what their media is, paint, stories, dance, woodworking, music. You create everyday, you create a life. Does that life reflect the artist within? Have you found a way to apply your imagination? You are already creating a life, now it is time to bring some passion, some imagination, some grace into the world.

I believe that finding your creative outlet is the best way to find "you". Does that mean you have to drop everything, abandon your job and family and go paint in Key West? No, not everyone who discovers their creative side has to abandon their life. No, your life experience makes you unique, you simply need to make time to let you... be you.

Why art? Because tapping into your experience, your imagination and freeing your creative beast is a way to recreate your life, how cool would it be to have something that you wait to get up and do everyday? I'd like to help you rediscover your passion for life again and I believe the shortest path is through creativity.

Someone asked me recently: "Am I really an artist or am I just tired of working?" The thought occurs to me too, playing in the sandbox is more fun than working with the grownups. Am I really an artist or have I created the world's best excuse for screwing around? We all get tired of working, but the question struck a deeper, more uncomfortable chord. Jackson Browne asked a similar question in a song I first heard in 1977, The Pretender:

"And believe in whatever may lie, in those things money can buy. Thought true love could have been a contender, are you there? Say a prayer for the pretender, who start out so young and strong, only to surrender."

There are times that this song keeps me awake at night. I wasn't going to become the Pretender. The question reminds me that the real work, the work I was sent here to do, has taken a backseat to the work I do to make money.

Ah the laughter of the lovers
As they run through the night
Leaving nothing for the others
But to choose off and fight
And tear at the world with all their might
While the ships bearing their dreams
Sail out of sight

Ooops.

Somewhere, the struggle for the legal tender took over, I AM the Pretender and don't think it doesn't piss me off to know it. Before I rented myself a house on the side of the freeway, I was religious studies major, I believed I could figure out this whole God thing and make the world a better place through my words, I could have been a contender. Of course I ended up being a stockbroker. I've had the perks and I've known, every minute of every day, that I was "selling out".

"I've been aware of the time going by, they say the end is the wink of an eye."

So yea, it hurts. Some days it hurts a lot, that's where Middle Aged Crazy comes from, I'm asking what a lot of us have asked, Am I really an artist? Mid life (and don't we hope this is only mid life?) is a good time to ask some pretty important questions. Like, when do I get around to making my soul happy? When do I get to be me?

What is this artist thing anyway? I played baseball back in the time the Pretender was written. Was I good enough to play professionally? Not hardly. But, I played baseball (not softball) until I was 45 years old, I was a ballplayer. I'm not going to the Hall of Fame (unless a I buy a ticket) yet I was a ballplayer nonetheless. So why is it the term artist is reserved for those who get paid for their creations? (There's the "things that money could buy" thing again. Artists have to deal with the struggle for the legal tender more than most.)

There is a member of my Improv Troupe who is wheelchair bound, she can only move from the neck up. I LOVE to do scenes with her, she is funny, creative, a great listener and humble. No one is going to tell me she is not an artist. Will she get rich at Improv? Not likely; Jennifer, like the rest our company, lives for her few minutes of creative comedy each week and I am inspired by her grace. She is an artist.

Let's get this straight: **if you create with emotion and inspiration, you are an artist.** (There; I've said it, it's up to you to make it your own truth). Let's not let that legal tender stuff cause us to decide who we are *any longer*. There's a lot of famous artists who didn't get paid for their work while they were alive, it's about the creation, not the things that money can buy. The fact is, we are all given equal amounts of grace and inspiration, there is no license required.

"I want to know what became of the changes we waited for love to bring."

Love is under a lot of pressure. We expect a lot from love. I read this from Deepak Chopra: "You were created to be completely loved and completely lovable for your whole life." That's pretty simple and pretty overwhelming, isn't it?

We didn't have to get all the things money can buy, didn't have to become the Pretender, we were already lovable as is, right out of the package. Then we surrendered (Ok, I surrendered). Love, which is our natural state, seems to slip away, we let fear and ego trick us into thinking we are not enough. The thing is, creation is an act of love.

You are enough. You are an artist when you bring your life experience, your joy and your passion to your day. When you tell your unique story, through any medium, you are an artist, even if that medium is your boring day job.

Being The Pretender by day allows me to create by night and now that I have figured this out, I'm not nearly as haunted. The struggle for the legal tender is no longer about status, about impressing people with my cash, about buying shiny gadgets (Ok, the IPad does look pretty cool). It's about enabling me to do "this", making a bunch of money doing "this" is only useful in that it will allow me to do more of "this". My soul is happy when I do "this".

So, be a creator. Be an artist. Be love. It's time.

Chapter 3 Exercises

Creativity= _____ _____

Creative People create. What do you wish you could create?

Where do your talents lie?

What was your favorite creative pursuit as a child?

Meditation: Can you get quiet and ask your soul to talk to you? What would make your soul happy?

There are four questions of value in life... What is sacred? Of what is the spirit made? What is worth living for, and what is worth dying for? The answer to each is the same. Only love." Don Juan deMarco

4 Is Your Well Empty?

Ray's Story: "I have to tell you, I was a pretty miserable guy, just a little while ago. I was frustrated at work, I felt like my life was slipping away, like I was reading from someone else's script. I'd come home, have a drink, bark some orders at my kids and fall asleep watching TV. Then get up in the morning and start all over again, some treadmill! It's funny but, playing guitar has actually given me and the kids something to talk about, I even played a little with my son. The writing has been a great outlet for me to, I don't feel quite as frustrated after I write down some of the things that happened during the day. I think more like a writer, like an artist now!"

Lynn's Story: "I went with my daughter to that rock concert, don't know who was more surprised by me offering to go, me or her! But, do you know what? Ever since I've started to paint again, I've come to appreciate contrast, there was certainly a lot of contrast at the concert. It wasn't the music I grew up with, but that's ok too, I appreciated the energy and the artistry. It's weird, but I find myself appreciating all manner of design and artistry now that I am creating stuff myself. All of my new experiences help me bring more color to my palette! I guess I am an artist now!"

Can you imagine a well for a minute? Not an oil well, but a water well, one that is there to provide for a whole village. Could this well give everyone in the village enough to drink and have enough left over for the crops if it is almost empty? No, a healthy well, one with abundance, with water overflowing is the one that can do the most good.

How is your well? If you are healthy, physically and emotionally, you are better suited to help those around you. Wouldn't you like your friends, family and co-workers see you as a happy, fulfilled person? I've talked with hundreds of people in the research for Middle Aged Crazy and I can tell you, this one is almost unanimous. We have taken on certain roles and responsibilities, our kids need us, our spouses need us, our clients need us. It's not like we have time to drop everything and sing anyway... So, we just go on, feeling a little empty, trying to keep our Creative Beast locked in a cage.

How effective are you when your well is empty? Are you at your best when you are in survival mode? Do your kids benefit from seeing you as always busy, always trying to catch up to life and out of control? Do your customers benefit from someone who only has time to do her job by the book? Most importantly how do you feel?

How do you feel when you are frustrated by all the things you don't have in life? How do you feel when you have no control? How do you like it when your life can be described by that horrible phrase, "Same shit, different day?" How effective are you when your well is empty?

Do you feel guilty? Guilt is such a wasted emotion. When you decide to approach life as an artist, you are not being selfish. You are making a choice to be a better parent, a better employer, a better employee, a better spouse. Choosing to release your creative beast makes your life fuller, more exciting and helps you to find meaning.

When you are living life like an artist you see more color, you have a greater understanding of contrast, you live with more passion, in short your well is full. When you have overflow, that's when you have enough for everyone. It's possible to approach "being You" in an attitude that will make life better for everyone around you.

I'd like to share what my particular version of being empty. My lesson in going through some darkness is that I have more to offer when my well is full. So do you. If you feel some of the things I'm about to describe, let me assure you, we are not alone!

By our middle years, a bunch of stuff can catch up to us. Decisions made along the way, decisions made in the interest of expediency and going with the flow can all of a sudden overwhelm you. Overwhelm (depression, feeling blue, call it what you want) is something that happens when you wonder if you've veered off into a dead end. When Overwhelm is here life is a movie and you are the audience. Words don't come to you, emotions are a memory, detachment and apathy seduce you into a sitting position, "I'll do that tomorrow." Inspiration can't penetrate Overwhelm, nothing does.

When Overwhelm gets here, you ride it out.

I've met some people who think you can tap on the back of your hand, your forehead and your ass, some nonsense called EFT, to get through overwhelm. These people are crazy. Overwhelm is about feeling powerless, about feeling hopeless, about feeling like you are another cog in the machine, you can tap yourself with a hammer and overwhelm won't go away.

Some people listen to God, or angels, or the other voices in their head, Overwhelm doesn't care who is talking, it smirks at all of them, calling bullshit on any thought that requires more action than pushing the remote button. Alcohol, a depressant, is Overwhelm's drinking buddy, it makes Overwhelm feel better. It tells Overwhelm it is sexy, funny and happy. Funny thing, even when overwhelm is feeling better, you know it's just overwhelm feeling better, not you. (Overwhelm likes cookies and fried food too, if it will let you eat at all.)

Goals, lists and activity can't penetrate overwhelm. Exercise would help but you can't drag yourself to the gym. The gym? Really, no I think this couch is much better.

Love might help, but, "what has love got to do with happiness?" (Jackson Browne). Love becomes a burden, something else to weigh you down. Overwhelm feeds on itself, it gets stronger, it whispers in your ear, "I will kill you." You have to decide if you can push through enough to thwart it. Sometimes you can't. You hope Overwhelm gets bored with you and lets you get up. It's pretty sad when you are too boring for Overwhelm.

Laughter is Overwhelm's enemy, so is teamwork. Enthusiasm kicks its ass, if it gains a foothold. Writing about Overwhelm seems to push it back into its hole a little; music works but the guitar is outside your bubble, you can't pick it up. Does singing the blues give you the blues or cure the blues? Overwhelm won't let you chance it.

"Faith, hope and love abide" said someone who had to deal with Overwhelm. Overwhelm says, "All at once or one at a time, I don't care, I'll lick you all."

When Overwhelm gets here, you ride it out. Riding it out is not something that happens in a vacuum. Your family sees you riding it out, they see you are not quite un-happy, but certainly not happy. They wonder if it is their fault, if they are disappointing you. Worse? Sometimes they don't even notice. If you are lucky, someone will ask, "What hurts?" If they really want to know, you might be able to tell them.

A while ago, I asked, "What hurts?" The answer I got was that creativity can help you deal with the hurt, that making something would help you deal with pain, that creation needs to be lubricated by emotion and pain is as good an emotion to draw upon as any. Sometimes, the pain wins and creating something is the furthest thing from your mind. What do you do?

I got a wonderful note one morning from a reader named Candy, an oncology nurse and I am pretty sure she understands pain better than I do. Candy said that creation eases pain, that expressing your pain lightens the load. Any emotion is better than going numb.

We'll do anything to avoid pain, yet pain is inevitable, it's part of being alive. I have given and received my share of pain. I have hurt people who love me, I have chosen a road that required me to face, ignore and cause pain. I have questioned everything, I have traveled the middle life highway. I have blamed other people for my emptiness, for I was lost. I have had a fog overtake me that everyone but me could see. Overwhelm is a big bad bear. Overwhelm is hell.

Middle Age, as I've said, is when we look back on a lifetime of decisions and wonder if the same decision making process will serve us in the future. In my case, I thought the answer might be "no". The journey has been harder on others than on me, I am sorry for the pain I've inflicted. I came to the conclusion that I had always taken the path of least resistance and I was leaving my light under a bushel. That damned Creative Beast was rattling the bars of his cage and making such a racket that I couldn't hear what was important, in my efforts to change my path, I did some damage. That damage didn't go unnoticed by me; it caused such confusion, doubt and uncertainty that I became a mannequin.

When "overwhelm" comes to town you don't want to write, don't want to listen to music, don't want to move: hope is gone. "What's the payoff?" Why make an effort to do anything if you are not going to come out in a better place? I can see why men my age take to the couch, where football and Nascar become our life.

Yet, I now see a light. It's hope again. Hope that the people I love will be Ok, that I can fix things, that I can help people with my words and actions. Playing guitar until my soul takes over for my fingers helps, seeing the look of love in others' eyes helps, giving my children a Father's love helps. I have hope now that I understand what love is, that I know what my life's mission is, that I have rescued myself from a path that was leading to a life of regret. Hope *is* way underrated.

Those that judge, that follow all the rules, that live by someone else's script have it easy when it comes to matters like these. Some of us are destined to wrestle with angels. Angels are tough opponents, they tell you what you don't want to hear, they insist you do things the right way. They give us glimpses of heaven and they take them away if we don't do things in integrity. I've had a taste of love, a taste of happiness, I wonder if that's all I'll get. Damn angels.

So, does creation save you? I think it does, creation comes from emotion, choosing to face emotion is better than being in that damned fog. And, as far as emotions go, pain is as good as any to draw from. Don Henley said, "Any kind of love without passion is no kind of loving at all."

So Angels, Bring it! I'll take you on, one at a time or all at once, it doesn't matter. I know you are trying to lead me out of the fog, to find my destiny, to be the person I came here to be. I'll fight you because I take the path of least resistance, because I will do anything to avoid pain, because I am scared. Because I am weak.
I know you are not, I know you will win, taking me to the finish line; fighting you all the way.

So, please, don't let your need to find yourself, to release your creative beast be derailed by love or by guilt. You deserve to take care of you. Your soul is talking to you, are you listening?

If love is your particular reason for not living to your passion, how much of a better example could you set for your kids, for your spouse, for your colleagues than by being an enthusiastic and engaged person?

Survival mode is a tough place to live for very long. Middle age is a time when we decide that simple survival is not enough. Think about what happens: You are born into the world as a helpless little creature. You are dependent on the help of others for the most basic things like food, water and a clean diaper. We learn to get along with people to best get those needs filled. Some of us learn to fight, some learn to please, some of us learn to smile and lick our lips...

As we grow, we make decisions based on our past experiences and what our environment teaches us. We make a series of decisions that lead us down a certain path, partly to survive, partly because that is what is expected of us. Go to college or don't. Get a job or live off the trust fund, we all learn to do what we need to do to survive. Our parents expect certain things from us, then our bosses do, then our kids. Along the way, we accumulate stuff, you know, appliances, couches, computers, mortgages, we end up with bills and on a treadmill, we pleasing others and living up to our obligations.

"Sure", we might remember, "a long time ago I took music lessons, I even practiced 4 hours a day, but where did that get me? Yea, someday I ought to get back to that, right after soccer practice and my 4 meetings today."

"Sure", we might remember, "someday I was going to take a cooking class, but you know what? I don't have the time or money for luxuries like classes. We'll just pick up a pizza on the way home."

The next thing you know, we are living out this unexciting script that we wrote. Survival is all we get to hope for. I'll pay the bills and watch a little TV, life is fine.

Survival mode is where alligators live; not people. When I fish in the pond near my home, the little Alligator who lives there asks a simple question when they he sees me, "Meat?" Alligators are beasts, they don't *have* a Creative Beast. Alligators don't have souls; they didn't come here on some existential mission. Survival mode is like that, it only asks one question "How do I benefit?" An alligator would probably say life is "fine."

By mid life, the treadmill is old, we realize we are meant to accomplish more than an alligator, we have something that we came here to do.

What? That's up to you, but it is more than the question, "Meat?" Suddenly, being "fine" isn't good enough.

When your well is full, you have more to teach, more love to give, more enthusiasm to share. Enthusiasm means "The God within." Enthusiasm is closer to fulfillment than an alligator ever gets. When you are passionate, when you bring excitement to your day, when your soul is truly happy, "fine" is never good enough again.

When you go through your day thinking like an artist, the people around you will notice. You will have more "spirit," more energy, your aliveness will be contagious. Will you be more emotional? God yes! Those emotions will be your tools, you'll notice little things all day long so you can use them later.

You'll learn to notice more detail, hear turns of phrases, taste more flavors, after all, you have something to create that day and who knows what might inspire you? You'll be surprised how just making your soul a little bit happy can chase Overwhelm away.

None of this needs to involve abandoning your role in life. (It might, but it doesn't *need* to). Guilt is not required simply because you want to find more meaning in your life. Sure, your relationships might need a adjusting. It's a good idea to tell people what you are doing. Again, coming from love is rarely a bad thing.

In most cases, the people in your life will be happy to let you try new things (or at least tolerate it). There are times when you realize relationships are getting in the way of your own growth. You may be too dependent on someone else to remember how to be you. Someone could be holding you back, you could be abused, lonely or in love with someone else. The people in your life, in some circumstances, might be threatened by any growth you exhibit.

Too bad. Rescuing your soul is your responsibility. Yours. If the people in your life don't want to play (or won't let you play) you don't get to quit. Get help if you need to, find support, take a class, join an internet group, go to Meetup.com, get counseling, but don't shut down. Please!

I think you'll find that life becomes richer once you move past "fine". Material possessions posses you less, televisions get turned off, you have less time for spectating.

Participating in your own life is a wonderful experience, it's what we were sent here to do.

How full is your well?

Chapter 4 Exercises

Draw a picture (or chart, graph, coffee cup painting etc.) of how empty (or full) you feel emotionally:

How do you think the people around you see you and your well?

Explain how Releasing Your Creative Beast will improve the life of everyone around you. (This is when you sell yourself).

Don't you wish you had a job like mine? All you have to do is think up a certain number of words! Plus, you can repeat words! And they don't even have to be true!
Dave Barry

• 5 Which Medium is Your Message?

Ray's Story: "Like I said, I've never really considered myself to be an artist. I've always loved music, but that's different than being a musician. I've picked up a guitar with the intention of learning how to play several times in my life but I never really had the discipline to follow through. I found out later, the used guitar I'd bought somewhere was set up all wrong for me and was very hard for a beginner to play. When I was 50, something happened, I decided I was tired of not being able to play and that I would learn, no matter how bad I sounded, no matter how hard it was. I've stuck to it for three years now and I can make enough music to make me happy. That's how I know the guitar is right for me, even if I don't sound anything like my records, I love it. Just playing a few chords still makes me happy! Writing is the same way, I never trained as a writer but I started a blog, the more I write, the more I want to write and I can see real improvement. Again, it makes me happy to think of myself as a writer.

Lynn's Story: In high school, before I got pregnant, I was really fascinated by art. I sort of put all that aside. A single Mom, with three kids has other priorities. While we were married, I'd sketch now and then, but we had other issues to deal with; developing my talent came behind the kids' needs and his demands. I sang in the choir at church, and I'd help the girls with their projects, so I still had a little taste of being an artist. One day, at church, they had an art class sign up. I'd always thought of a beginners' class as beneath me, I was, after all, an artist, but I signed up anyway, not sure why. I guess I had an inspiration. It was a great decision, I paint every day and Rachel has the gene too, she goes to class with me and we compare notes. I paint flowers, she paints, well, different stuff than I do. The important thing, we have both found a great outlet."

When we talk about attaining hopes and dreams, we try to avoid a place called "Someday Isle" You know, "someday I'll write a book", "someday I'll learn to play guitar", it's always someday I'll. Well, part of becoming You is deciding what your creative outlet is. Let's see if we can figure out what your new magnificent obsession is going to be, shall we?

There's a pretty good chance that you know what is calling you, that you have a pretty good idea of what you want to do, you simply need permission. If you've always known you are going to write, or paint then this part is easy, just give it a go! Like Ray, I have always known I was a writer, I wrote whenever I could for my job, I always volunteered to write newsletters for organizations, words and communications have always fascinated me. My calling was clear.

But, what if you aren't sure? There's probably a LOT of things you'd like to do and trying all of them would be exhausting, it's time to find out what is calling you. What's calling you will probably be something that comes somewhat easily to you, at least at first, talent is nice: but not required. Even the most naturally talented people still have to put in the time.

This is a good place to mention that shame is not a very good tool when it comes to selecting your creative outlet. Forget that Miss Arrigi, the most horrible person (and English teacher) on Earth said that you couldn't write or the choir instructor who told you not to sing. Don't start with lack, or, especially, this phrase, "I am not creative, at all." Once you udder those words, it takes your brain a while to forget them. I don't care if you are the most left brained tax attorney on the planet, you are creative. Let's not begin with what you can't do, *let's focus on what you'd really, really like to do!*

There's a really interesting book out called Talent is Over Rated (Geoffrey Colvin) and, when it comes to finding your creative outlet, it truly is. Talent is no more than this: something comes easily to you. Studies have shown that this can be a double edged sword: if something comes easily to you, the positive reinforcement you get from performing your outlet will lead to more practice, because you are enjoying yourself; a virtuous circle. The other side of the coin? You might be talented at something you don't feel strongly about, you might even be slightly bored by it.

Research has shown that it is the time you put in that counts more than natural talent. Someone who practices, puts in the hours is going to pass the talented person who doesn't practice, every time. Sure, we'd all like to be freaky talented and super motivated to get better, it just doesn't always work out that way for everyone.

Deciding to find a creative outlet to express your soul's passion is not as simple as writing a book the first time you sit down at a keyboard and turning it into a bestseller. It's not the same as sitting down with a cello and playing right along with a symphony. Of course not, it takes commitment and passion to learn something new as an adult, you'll know when you find your outlet because you'll be fascinated by it for life.

I believe, strongly, that you need to find a creative outlet that does three things:

1. Fascinates and challenges you.
2. Is something that you are motivated to do from inside.
3. Something that has meaning to you, it must touch your soul.

I'm going to talk more about these ideas, but it's time for a story. Did you know that Dave Matthews, singer, songwriter, and now famous rock star was a bartender? He'd written 4 songs and it took the urgings of one of his customers to get his music out there. He got up the courage to approach some local musicians he'd heard in the places he worked and they skeptically listened. "How should we play them?" "Well I like the way you play, so play it however you would interpret it."

Enter rock stardom, right this way please! Dave is a guy who couldn't contain his passion, who let his creative beast come out and play. His story is so full of lessons for someone who is where you are, he allowed for Grace.

I've been learning a very sad song, Grace is Gone, one Matthews wrote after his stepdad died. (Grace was a metaphor for their loving relationship.) Grace has been a theme in my work and the story of Dave Matthews' success fits in with the concept of finding your passion and having the faith to go with the feeling.

I'm a big believer in personal responsibility, creating your own success and putting yourself in the right environment. I have no time for toxic people, for cynics, for meanness. It's as easy to lift someone up as it is to put them down, so I find that my creativity is best nurtured in a nurturing environment. It's impossible to release your Creative Beast if you are a hermit and don't get some help; some grace. You get what you ask for, if you are surrounded by toxic people, you might want to find out if that's what you are putting out there. Getting help from supportive and loving people is one of my favorite forms of Grace.

The Dave Matthews story is quite a parable. First, he's a bartender, he's not a professor of music, not a Music Row executive, not some famous guy. He was the guy who fixed your rum and coke and got you a bag of Doritos from the black metal rack next to the lottery tickets. It's obvious now, but who knew he was a genius when he was wiping down the bar? It makes me wonder, how many talented people do you see everyday without knowing it? How many artists are delivering your packages, teaching in your kid's school or standing next to you in line at the movies? Do you look for the genius in people? In you?

The next part of the Dave story is he just had four songs. He didn't have a catalogue, he had FOUR songs when he got together with his band. He didn't wait for his work to be "finished" he had the faith in his inspiration to go with what he had. How many times have I let work die on the vine, waiting for it to get "finished"? Perfection is elusive and it's perfectly alright to put your work out there. Your message is your message, don't be too harsh a judge, waiting for perfection is just another form of procrastination. Creative resistance knows all of our weaknesses!

Next, it took a friend to encourage Dave to pursue his music dream. Dave was reluctant to play or sing his songs in front of others. Attorney Ross Hoffman, Dave's customer, convinced him to show his work to the folks who became the members of his band. Did you hear that? A now famous rock star was afraid to play his stuff for a local bar musician! It took the encouragement of a friend to bring out his music, to set him on the way to fulfilling his destiny. Don't you wish you had a friend who believed in you so strongly that he was willing to push you out of your comfort zone? Wouldn't it be great if you could do that for someone? Today Dave is a famous singer, singing his work and that of others' and he was reluctant to sing at all! Thank you Grace, for friends!

Next lesson? Dave trusted his fellow musicians. Trust and teamwork are a big part of success, success is a team sport. Dave realized that his musician friends were good enough to interpret his work and let them have the creative freedom to make his songs their own. When I am tempted to show I am the smartest guy in the room, it's nice to remember to breathe a little and listen. Sometimes collaboration is just what the doctor ordered. The Dave Mathews band, born of this collaboration, is still together, making music as a very successful team.

Even the song Grace Is Gone has a graceful ending. After Dave recorded the song a recording label executive pronounced it to be too sad for his album. The song was relegated to the place unrecorded songs go, right next to rejected manuscripts and unmet dreams. The song got out to fans anyway and became a staple of his shows. Grace was the centerpiece of an album of other rejected songs, Busted Stuff, a year later, one of the band's best works. Grace abounds, it can't be hidden in a closet forever.

So, no, I don't have the time or energy to waste on those who think grace is a myth, who think giving is another form of enabling. Giving encouragement, learning to trust, helping each other to rise up is why I founded Middle Aged Crazy and I am so happy to see that so many people are connecting and encouraging each other through this project. After all, if one of the most successful performers in our times was willing to ask for a little help from his friends, who am I to be a hermit?

What else? When help is offered, when inspiration shows up, when Grace is everywhere, you have to *allow it and accept it*. Dave did, otherwise, he'd still be getting your refills. How are you at asking for help? How about receiving? How do you feel about letting a little inspiration into your life?

What's this all got to do with finding your passion in life and your creative outlet? Trust your feeling, your instinct and go with it. Ask for some help, be willing to learn, don't worry about making everything perfect.

Here's an important thing, if you find your true creative outlet, you won't mind having to learn and master a new field, it will seem like play. Sure, learning a new skill is part of the deal, but you'll know when you've found your perfect outlet because even the learning is fun and fascinating. When you find something you love, you'll be excited to learn to do it, you'll consider practice to be "play" and you'll look forward to learning the next step.

In my case, I can't wait to write, I wake up thinking of things to tell you and I can't stop thinking of things until I pass out from exhaustion at night. Dancers are always moving, painters always see scenes, musicians find music in the sound of the wind. If you could call yourself any kind of artist, what would you most like to be called? Actor, writer, chef? There's power in words, try a few on and see how they sound on you! Play the game I played in the airport, what feels right?

When you find a means of expression that fascinates and challenges you; you feel that you might never completely master your medium. All artists are driven by a curiosity and fascination with their medium, the right medium will fascinate you for the rest of your life, you'll feel like you always have just a little more to learn, just a little more before you have really mastered it.

The more you learn, the more you'll appreciate the work of others and realize, while you are improving, you are not in any danger of being bored. At the same time, your medium will let you jump right in and express yourself, even if you have just started. (New artists have some advantages).

By the way, this is as good a time as any to tell you some semi- bad news. If you are trying to find your creative outlet to replace your current job (and you are starting from scratch as a beginner), please don't! In the first place, once you put that kind of pressure on your creative beast, he will freak out and give you that ulcer you were trying to avoid anyway. Second, if you are meant to be the next great writer or painter (or whatever) your genius will speak for itself and the right people will find you.

Recent studies have told us that creativity actually decreases as soon as you assign a monetary goal to the creative outcome. Middle Aged Crazy might lead you to a new career which involves your new found skill, but, keep in mind, it takes about 10,000 hours to truly master a new skill. It might be an easier goal to use your new found creativity to improve your existing job. Yes, Dave Matthews had 4 songs: he didn't quit his bartending job until the band had steady work.

YOUR calling. Remember when your parents dragged you to oboe lessons? Some kids lucked out, they liked the lessons. Some kids didn't, they really wanted to play a screaming electric guitar, or they didn't like music at all. The lessons weren't a wonderful opportunity, they were punishment! What is your calling, what creative pursuit is calling you?

Psychologists have found that you have to be autonomous to be a successful creative. Getting dragged to oboe lessons isn't going to cut it. Now that you are an adult, you can re-visit those childhood lessons and decide if you have an interest in getting re-acquainted or if you are being called to create through a different medium.

Your means of expression must have some kind of meaning to you, you simply have to feel like you are expressing yourself in a way that makes your life (or someone else's better). Your creative outlet must make your soul happy or you will, eventually, give up on it. (I'm not saying giving up, sampling new crafts and finding different means of expression is a bad thing. Not at all; I am saying that when you find one of your true creative outlets, it will be something you can't stop doing.) When you find your voice, you become a very powerful being. Mastering a new creative outlet gives you power to your voice, it makes your point of view MATTER!

- It's not the dance, not the painting, not the words, not the statue, not the symphony:
- IT'S WHAT THE DANCE, THE PAINTING, THE STATUE AND THE SYMPHONY SAY! (me)

If you have read this chapter and still don't know what your outlet is, that's ok, you don't have to decide right now. Here are a few ideas:

1. Remember what you did as a child, what was your favorite thing to do? What do you gravitate towards, who did you admire?

2. Meditate. Seriously, get quiet, pray, ask your soul for help.

3. Sample: Look for local groups, ask friends, find a cool class.

Getting creative is about finding your voice, your ways to express your passion, your rage, your drama, your love.

What DO you have to say?

Chapter 5 Exercises

What emotions trigger your desire to create?

Your creative outlet should feel like a never ending puzzle. What are all of the things you'd like to learn and master about your chosen creative media?

Let's pretend you are starting a new creative career today and money is no object. What would you like your day to look like?

How could you find meaning from your creative pursuit?

Homework: Do a Google Search of like minded people, classes, instructors and groups in your area. (Hint: start with Meetup.com)

There are very few monsters who
warrant the fear we have of them.
~Andre Gide

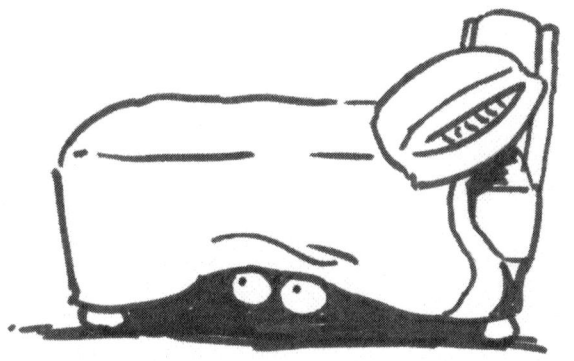

· 6 It's Ok To Be Afraid

Ray's Story: You know what is really weird? The first time I took a guitar lesson I was really nervous. Like I had stage fright, it was so bad that I couldn't play in front of the teacher. I just let him show me stuff and play on his own guitar. What was that all about? You know, I even play real quietly around the house so no one makes fun of me. I hear the improvement but I don't know if anyone else would appreciate it. I guess I'm not used to being wrong about things, not used to making mistakes. As a parent, as a businessman, I am supposed to get things right. This creative stuff is quite a stretch for me. I'm happy I've taken this road, I've learned that it is ok to be a little uncomfortable.

Lynn's Story: My friends sell their art at fairs. I don't know about that, I'm not ready. I mean, who would buy my stuff? I'm afraid if it I put it out there, it would change the way I feel about doing the work. I paint because it makes me happy, not because I want to be judged. Sure my girls like what I do, but, I'm going to need a little convincing before I let someone else see what I do. I'm putting myself out there and the last thing I need to do is face rejection over it. No, I'm happy to paint and feel good about for me. Maybe someday I'll require an audience, but not now.

Fear...

This one is real...

Very real.

One of the hardest things we have to deal with is the fear that once we actually do something, we might not be very good at it.

It's one thing to say, "Someday I'll write a book."

It's something completely different to sit in front of a blank computer screen with no idea what to do next. There's that little chill that starts in the back of your head, "Oh My God" I guess I am in over my head now!"

It's one thing to promise yourself that you will take piano lessons someday...

It's something completely different to find yourself sitting next to a music teacher. "Well, he plays so well and my fingers won't do what I want them to. Rhythm, what's that? I just wanted to play a few notes of American Pie, now I am supposed to learn scales?"

Even the most talented creative has to deal with demons like stage fright, why should you be any different? Writers block, stage fright and all of their evil cousins are simply versions of self editing. Self editing is that thing our ego does to protect us from rejection. I have sent manuscripts out and mentally composed my own rejection letter, saving the publisher the trouble.

"Someday" is nice, it is a dream.

A pleasant thought, sort of like spending all that lottery money right after you buy the ticket. The thing about dreams, is they are perfect. We refine them, we shape them, we know our book will be picked up by a publisher, it will be loved by the critics, it will become a bestseller. We don't write a script for failure into our dreams.

Then there's that awful phrase again, "Let's be realistic." Being realistic *is* awful sometimes, especially when it comes to be being creative. Walt Disney was famous for letting his imagination and dreams take over, money was truly no object to him. (It was to his brother Roy who had to figure out how to finance all of Walt's dreams). This child of the depression, paper boy, Army Ambulance driver created an entertainment empire because he refused to be realistic. If Walt had a fear of failure, he kept it to himself. Most of us have to confront fear to create and not everyone is a big fan of confrontation.

And it's not like we are sitting there worrying about failure, no, it's just in the back of our minds, just this little unsettling thought. "What if I can't do it?" In our script, we sit down at the piano and effortlessly play a Christmas Carol, no, a medley of Christmas carols for everyone we know. Only, when we ACTUALLY sit down at the piano, we are lucky if chopsticks comes out... That feeling of being SO new, so incompetent, is something you probably haven't felt since childhood. It's like the more we imagined ourselves being great at something, the harder it is to be a beginner.

And, let's face it, there are enough other reasons to put off your project, "I don't have time", "I have more practical things to do", I really should spend more time on my work"... So, we don't ever have to face that fear... Did I say fear? I meant that certainty, that we are not good enough. Why would we be good enough? We've been raising kids and making money, not learning a new art technique! We'd like to think it is money for nothing and chicks for free, then we pick up the guitar! "How Do they get any sound out of this thing?"

Our brain has already written the rejection letter from the publisher, already written the bad reviews from the critics, already pictures our book in the "Buy 2 get one free bin" Oh yea, resistance love to strangle us at this stage. "Why waste your time at something else you will suck at?"

Can I help you with this phase of resistance?

First, I'd like you to remember this rather inelegant phrase:

"Allow yourself to suck!"

Let this be your new motto, revel in your suckage! When you are new at something, anything, you are not expected to be a master, so own it! Take joy in every little baby step you make forward, release the pressure! For maybe the first time since you were in pre-school, revel in failure, in ineptitude, in the joy of not being an expert. Own it!

Google says they don't want their employees to be afraid to "make a big mistake". Most of us don't work in that supportive an environment, we are expected to make no mistakes, big or small. No one wants a brain surgeon who isn't afraid to make the big mistake. There are things like malpractice suits and compliance departments to keep us away from making mistakes, we've been told there is a "correct" answer since we were in Kindergarten.

Guess what? Your creative pursuit is not brain surgery! Have fun, screw up, take chances. There is no right answer to releasing your beast. There's not even a curve. You get to decide the curriculum, you get to grade you, so don't be Miss Arrigi! Relax, if it takes you 3 months to be able to move your left hand from one chord to another on your guitar, so what? (True story, sorry to admit!)

I'd like to recommend a really good book called the War of Art, author Steven Pressfield identifies *creative resistance* as the enemy and gives you many strategies for powering through fear and getting your work done. It is resistance that tells you to give up, that you have better things to do, that you are too old to learn something new, resistance is your enemy and it knows all your weaknesses.

Resistance says, go ahead, one more Krispy Kreme to the guy who just started a diet. Resistance tells you to stop practicing your guitar for the sake of your family's ears, it tells you sit down and watch the rest of the movie, you can write later. Resistance is your evil foe, the enemy of creation. Resistance tells you to stop before you make a fool of yourself. At least that's what he told me. I have a self editor and he's a nice enough guy, nice enough for an agent of the devil.

I call my editor the Brakeman. Met him during a meditation a few years ago, he had been keeping me from singing out loud. All it took was someone whose opinion I value to say, "You were off key" and the Brakeman took over, he made sure I wasn't off key for the next ten years; I developed a phobia about singing in public. (I'm no Pavarotti, but I can carry a tune, sound a little like James Taylor.) I picture him as this old time train conductor, generated from the left side of my brain and making sure, in his words, "that you don't make a fool of yourself, AGAIN."

He was born when I got my first pimples. Yup, I was about fourteen when I looked in the mirror and he first spoke up, "God, that is hideous, you look awful." And, I gave him power, I listened to him. He was there when I tried to call a girl for a date, when I wrote my first college essay, when I tried to speak to people who were older and richer. He caused my nervous laugh, my sarcasm, my anger. He was there to keep me in line, to make sure no one saw me for the fool he knew I truly was.

My Brakeman made sure that I was always "right"; he didn't let me make mistakes, even if that meant not trying new things. He was firmly against creativity, unless it was writing, because he could edit my words on the screen. Dance spontaneously? Participate in exercises that might show your true feelings and emotions? Tell someone when you are afraid?

Not going to happen. My Brakeman was going to make sure that I was never going to be vulnerable, he was the keeper of the train, making sure I stayed on schedule. He was the Left Brain's hired gun, sent to keep an eye on that dangerous Right Side, the other side of the tracks. He made sure I was a "Man." He made sure everyone knew I was the smartest guy in the room, someone who was never "wrong".

Like I said, I met him during a meditation led by Hale Dwoskin using something called the Sedona Method. It's a simple process: you realize that resisting something gives it power, so you stop fighting it. I went into the meditation wondering why I couldn't sing any more and I kept going deeper and deeper until I came face to face with The Brakeman. He was nice enough, "he really does want to protect me". I thanked him for the job he was doing and told him how I appreciated him looking out for me.

I told him that I wasn't fourteen anymore and that I could stand to make just a little bit of a fool of myself. Despite his best efforts, I'd done that anyway and it proved to be embarrassing but not fatal. I asked him to ease up on the brakes, that I needed to grow. He grumbled for a while but I was finally able to imagine, as Hal would say, "just for a minute to see what life would be like without him holding the brake". And, for just a minute, I could imagine it. Once you can imagine something for a second, it's not a big leap to live it forever. Being present is a nice little trick.

Just like that, the Brakeman was retired and an hour later, I was on stage at the conference I was attending, singing with a Nashville songwriter, Jana Stanfield. I went from not being able to sing *in* the middle of a group of 400 to being able to sing *in front* of the group of 400 because I met and retired the Brakeman.

Am I a performer? Not hardly, I haven't sung in public again and I don't plan to. But, I have been able to realize what the Brakeman has been doing to me. He'd ask questions like, "Will anyone read this steaming turd you are typing?" "Is this how you are supposed to write a book?" "You have no credentials, you'll never get a publisher to buy this, are you nuts?" "You aren't a professional speaker, you are quiet, you are self conscious. Why would anyone come to hear you?"

He still asks those questions but I know it is "him" now and not me. He is the one who writes the rejection letter before I send in the proposal, the one who "hates my voice" on tape, the one who tells me I have nothing new to say. He is still trying to protect me from going to far out on a limb.

And I love him, but like one would with an over protective Parent, I have learned to make my own way, to climb out on a limb and bring the chainsaw with me.

It's made all the difference.

I hope you'll thank your Brakeman and let him live the rest of his days in Sun City while you Release your Creative Beast!

Remember how I said no one can write your book or sing your song? They can't. But YOU can. It comes down to a matter of redefining success and failure. Stop putting all these ridiculous conditions on your creative beast.

You wouldn't dream of going up to a new piano student and saying, "You better be good enough to play Carnegie Hall by this time next year." Yet, we do it all the time to ourselves.

The bookstores are full of books by authors who just wanted to tell a story or explain something in their own words. There's a book out there called The Shack. It's a religious book and it might not be your cup of tea (or it might). Besides the message *in* the book, the story *of* the book is inspirational.

William P. Young was a church volunteer handyman who came up with a story about his understanding of God for his family. He'd run off a few copies of the story and after a few friends read it, he started to get more requests. He went to Kinko's and fashioned a little book he sold to friends to cover his cost. And the demand kept growing until some of his friends from church helped him create a publishing company LLC. They started to sell a few copies.

The Shack's popularity grew until the little book became a New York Times bestseller! Young is now a minor celebrity and considered something of a theologian, by everyone but himself. He still thinks of himself as a Dad who wanted to explain God to his daughters. He said yes to inspiration and allowed creation to flow through him. His chosen media: words. He wrote a wonderful book. He didn't set out to become a famous author or make a bunch of money; he simply had a story to tell. I don't think he stopped to think long enough to let fear wander in, he simply told a story. His story.

The best way to write your book? The best way to play your song? Start. It's that simple. Here's an important lesson I've learned from meeting a few famous authors: The difference between an author and you? He wrote a book. That's it, he doesn't breathe rarified air or eat spinach from a can like Popeye. He wrote, he told his story.

You have something to say, you have stories to tell. And today, with the advent of the internet, you will find an audience. Why would you let someone else judge the truth of your experience or the quality of your work? Your Beast isn't telling you to create, "if it is okay with everyone else." He doesn't really care if you have an audience at all.

Because, I have to tell you, no matter how talented or creative you are, there will be people who don't like your work. So what?
If you are feeling fulfilled, if you are getting your story out there, who cares what anyone else thinks? My experience has been that people are a lot more accepting and interested in good work than you might think.

If you have something to say and say it with passion through your work, you will find your audience. And if you don't? So what? Middle Aged Crazy isn't about quitting your job and becoming a full time artist. Sure, that might happen, but we are talking baby steps. First you need to create something, then see if fame, fortune and great critical reviews show up!

Here's another little secret: when you let your creative beast out, you begin to see yourself and the entire world differently. You begin to think and act like an ARTIST. That's a pretty cool place to live. Artists see the world differently, they are always in touch with source, they are always open to inspiration... Let's talk about that inspiration thing next. It's way cool!

Chapter 6 Exercises

Your dream: What is your creative dream? Is it to write a best selling book that changes the world or simply take some beautiful photo's to hang on your wall? Forget "reality" just write (or draw) your dream, no holding back, make it beautiful!

Ok, now in really small print, write down all of the things you are afraid of. (I'll get rejected, I'll suck at it, my spouse will laugh at me, etc.)

Now that you've written them down, don't most of them seem kind of silly? Which ones can you laugh off and which ones can you work with? How much creativity are you holding back on because of money reasons?

.

"Sometimes you've got to let everything go – purge yourself. If you are unhappy with anything . . . whatever is bringing you down, get rid of it. Because you'll find that when you're free, your true creativity, your true self comes out."
Tina Turner

7 Finding Inspiration

Ray's Story: "You know the funny thing about my writing? I am never at a loss for something to write about. Some days, as soon as the shower water hits my head a blog starts to compose itself. By the time I get to the computer, it is all written, I just have to type it out. I used to worry that I'd forget it if I didn't get it out in time, I'd rush to the computer without stopping for coffee. Now I am calmer about that, I know it will be there for me. It's weird, but some of the best stuff I've written hasn't been written by me, if you know what I mean. I'm almost channeling it. I've learned to look for that feeling and to trust it. The guitar feels that way too, some nights. I get into a groove and it almost feels like my guitar would keep playing if I took my hands off it. That's pretty cool!"

Lynn's Story: "I've always been in touch with spirit. My girls think I am a little crazy, but they know I believe I am surrounded by angels. When I paint, they are there to guide me. Mom's are pretty intuitive, I think, and I have really started to rely on my sixth sense. I seem to know when my kids need me or when they are going to call. It's that way when I paint too, I just try to tell a story with my brush and things seem to paint themselves. It's like I am in a trance, a wonderful, calming, trance."

We used to call it women's intuition, remember? My Mom seemed to know who was on the phone before she answered it and that's what she'd call it, "Women's intuition." I think we've taken the gender label out of it, but there is no denying, some people seem to be more intuitive than others. In my research, I've found that inspiration is everywhere, if you learn to plug into it.

Intuition and inspiration are pretty closely related, they are both voices that we can't deny or explain. Both words have their roots in the Latin for Divine Inspiration. When you are in touch with source, inspiration is never far away, it seems to be a matter of paying attention. The more you practice your chosen creative craft, the more you'll be in touch with inspiration.

In my book, The Affluent Artist, I interviewed a famous Hollywood psychic, Joanna Garzilli, and she claims that being more intuitive is just a matter of "plugging in", that we are all capable of being psychics". Joanna's clients are known to call her before they decide to go ahead with movie projects, they value her ability that much. Joanna's doesn't consider her gift to be supernatural as much as she considers it "developed." The more you plug into intuition, the more you will receive it.

I predict that you can become more creative by plugging into intuition. The ancient Romans used to call it your "genius," they believed that inspiration for creative endeavors came from outside of you, you simply made yourself available to it. Somewhere along the way, we have come to believe that inspiration is internally generated, that it is something that comes from within. This idea is commonly excepted with almost everyone except truly creative people.

I have interviewed hundreds of gifted artists and I can tell you, most of them believe their creations come from someplace beyond their body. They all describe the feeling slightly differently, they say they are "channeling" or they are the "Instrument" or "I just heard it." Universally, they consider inspiration a gift and they aren't all sure how or when it will arrive again. Some of them don't even like to discuss inspiration, least it never visit again.

Inspiration can come from within or from an outside stimulus, it's a little different for everyone. Everyone has their own little creative routine (or discipline). Many creatives have a disciplined approach, they know if they follow a certain routine inspiration will usually show up. Think about professional artists, they can't wait for the right mood to strike, they have to create to keep their jobs. They simply try to create the right environment for "Flow" to appear.

Flow is that feeling you get when you are so deep in creation that the ideas are flowing to you, everything is almost in slow motion and you don't hear someone who comes in the room to talk to you. Flow is a wonderful place, athletes talk of experiencing it, the devout religious can feel it, some know it, however briefly in the passions of sex and: artists go into flow. Not only do artists know flow, they seem to be able to sustain this level of consciousness longer than any of the other people who experience it. (Told you being an artist was cool!)

How do you do that? By saying "Yes" to inspiration. Sometimes inspiration is subtle, sometimes it screams at you, you'll have to learn how to discern it. So many times we get a creative idea and squish it before it comes to fruit. "No I can't do that" or "That's silly". When, in reality, nothing happens, creatively or not, until we say "Yes" to an inspiring idea.

I've mentioned that I am an Improvisational Comedy performer and, as a warm up, we play a game called "Yes and..." In this Improv game, no idea, no matter how ridiculous, is ever turned down. The death of an Improv scene is when someone declines an offer and ruins the illusion another actor has created. Improv has one hard and fast rule; "Everything is true." So, if I say to a fellow performer, "Well doctor, it looks like I have this cabbage stuck on my foot," the scene is dependent on my partner saying, "Yes, and we'll need to operate." If she says, "no, I'm not a doctor" or, "That's silly, there is no cabbage on your foot," the scene is probably going no where. Saying "Yes and..." is the key to creating a funny scene.

It turns out that inspiration is a lot like Improv, the more you say "YES" the more it shows up. When you release your creative beast, you find inspiration everywhere, it becomes part of your day. We know that creativity best comes from an emotion, so, as you go through your day, you'll notice yourself filing the various emotions you experience away for later use. In my experience, I stay more "present" and don't let my emotions carry me away as much as they once did. Creativity as helped me to observe my emotions and decide which ones I can use and which ones I don't need. (For an emotional Italian/French hybrid like me, this is some trick!)

Everyone has a lot of creative ideas, but that doesn't make you "creative". "Creation" by definition, is about making something. If you have a lot of ideas; you are a day dreamer. If you have a lot of ideas and make some of them real: you are an artist. As we said, creation = applied imagination. Plugging into the imagination part is a great first step to becoming an artist.

How do you find this inspiration? Everyone has their own process and it is important that you find yours. I know a few things that work, and one is to find something that you feel strongly about. Emotions are the window to your soul and I find that I create best when I have a strong emotion to work with. Find something that annoys you, or something that you feel another strong emotion about and go with it. Listen to some of your favorite songs and think about how all the good lyrics come from a strong feeling, how the best stories draw you in with feelings you identify with, how the best art makes you want to go live in the painting.

Buying paintbrushes, wood for your workshop or paper for your printer indicates a certain level of faith that something is going to make the transition from thought to reality. How does one create a new piece of work, a new reality? *Magic*. That magic involves reaching into the dark closet where we keep the creative stuff, how do you know you'll pull the right creative tool off the shelf? Trust...

Perhaps the biggest lesson I've learned on my journey into creativity is that of trust. It's a word that comes up over and over, "Trust the feeling", "Trust the intuition", "Trust your partner". It takes a certain amount of courage to trust and understand that nothing creative happens until you journey into the unknown, that's where the magic happens.

I just finished a guitar lesson with my guitar teacher and, we've figured out that the best way for me to improve is to jam. We'll alternate rhythm and lead in a certain key and just go, improvising the whole way. His message is to trust your instinct, to go with the rhythm. We are learning, as a duo, to trust each other. Granted, he's been playing for 34 years and I've only been playing for about 3, we still reach a certain level of understanding through the music, sometimes will end up playing a certain phrase together at the same time, almost like we knew it was the right thing to do. The more we play together, the better we'll get (mostly because I have no where to go but up) and it is exciting to get on that level of trust with such a good musician. Trust the music...

One evening I went to the Orlando Improv Festival and witnessed trust like I've seldom seen it. In a 2 man show called, "Is This Seat Taken?", Jay Hopkins and David Charles, two Improv veterans, with 4 audience prompts and two chairs, bravely constructed a 45 minute one act play. Even though I enjoy Improv, I secretly cringed at the idea of sitting through my first "long form" Improv, thinking, "this will be beyond uncomfortable." I was pleasantly mistaken. The show moved quickly, we ended up caring about the characters and the situation they found themselves in. We were actually disappointed when the show ended. What was my lesson? Trust. The two actors truly trust one another, how else could you get on stage if you didn't know your partner was going down the same stream with you? Trust your fellow artists...

In my own Improv class the next Sunday, we had "teacher evaluations" and Professore' Charles told me he was a big fan of mine. His suggestion, (here's that word again) "trust my instincts." He wanted me to have the confidence to go big, to take my first thought and play it up, to not be quite so tentative. Trust your gut...

Admittedly, performing arts lend themselves more to improvisation, to the unexpected, but all creativity requires a certain leap of faith. Skill is important, so is talent and desire. Natural ability and deciding to create something is very scientific, left brained and clinical until you add magic. Creation is not reproduction, creative instinct requires you climb out on a limb with a chainsaw, knowing that you'll be just fine... somehow. Trusting your fellow cast members, your training and your own instinct is how you find the magic. The magic is speaking up in silence, it's taking action on an idea, it's the confidence to know that you have tapped into genius.

Remember, genius is something you borrow, and to plug into this particular vein of gold, you need to have the courage to go with the feeling... to trust.

As we've established; art only happens as a result of an emotion being communicated. Some artists paint, some use words, some dance, some macramé. No matter what the media, nothing artistic happens until someone feels strongly about something and decides to tell us about it. What do you feel strongly about?

Learning a new craft is a technical exercise until you put feeling in it. The Blues and Rock and Roll are pretty much based on 3 simple chords. It's the feeling that comes through the music that makes it art. There are some excellent ONE chord rock and roll songs (i.e. We Will Rock You by Queen.) Does playing that one chord over and over create a song? Nope. Playing that chord from your soul, with passion, can make it a classic. You need that Magic.

You don't have to master your media to excel in it. The most technically correct pieces are no more than exercises if they don't communicate an emotion. (The song Life in The Fast Lane by the Eagles was a Joe Walsh warm up exercise until Don Henley and Glenn Frey heard Walsh warming up and applied a little passion.) With practice, lessons and hard work won't you improve, technically, at your chosen craft? Of course, but, if you get to the point where feeling is no longer an integral part of your work, you have downgraded yourself from artist to technician.

The guy who remodels your kitchen might be a great craftsman. He can technically follow every detail of the blueprints. Is he an artist? (I'll admit I don't know, it is difficult to argue over who is an artist, it's a lot like arguing over which devout church goer is a better Christian, it's a fairly unimaginative argument.) My inclination is that the person who imagined the kitchen and drew the blueprints is the actual artist. Technical skill requires its own creativity and magic, for the sake of my argument, the person who imagined where the cutting board goes, what type of sink fixtures look best and what colors to paint the walls has done more "creating." The designer imagined the kitchen as a living, functional space, she thought about things like traffic flow, aesthetics and chopping onions. She might have imagined the happy (and sad) times that families experience in their kitchen. I'm sure she drew on her own emotions and experiences in coming up with her design.

Someone posted on the Middle Aged Crazy Facebook page something to the effect of, "Goodbye Beast, tired of the drama." I'm not sure what drama she was referring to, someone's good discussion can be someone else's whining. We do share a little emotion on this page and I appreciated her point of view. The thing is, I don't think I can fix it, it is impossible to create without emotion.

Artists emote.

Artists without emotion are technicians, craftsmen. As skilled as they might be, until skilled craftsmen bring something of their own to a project they are not artists. If you get really good at paint by numbers, you may be perfecting technique and becoming better at your craft; but it's a stretch to say you are an artist until you paint something of your own. (I realize, in proof reading, that I'm talking about more than art here, how many of us go through life as if it is paint by numbers; filling in the colors someone else has designated?)

We keep coming back to this one: "Creation is applied imagination." I stumbled upon this definition a few months ago and realized that it says it all. Someone with a good imagination is just that, someone with a good imagination. Nothing wrong with that, imagination is awesome, but until you tie a verb to it you are simply a daydreamer. We have millions of thoughts and ideas, which ones get you off the bench? The ones you feel strongly about (you are pissed, you are in love, you lonely) are the ones that lead to the best work.

Angst is part of creation too: Will anyone like my work? Did I have the technical skill to pull it off? Am I going a little too far this time? Am I revealing too much this time? When you really come from a creative place you are putting yourself out there, putting your soul on the line. Not everyone can do that.

I dreamed one morning that I was in a one hundred person Improv, we were supposed to create this flash mob Improv thing. Only no one had the guts to say anything, the entire exercise was a failure. Everyone, including me, decided it was better to remain silent than take a chance on being wrong. (And I think you know where I stand on Mimes. I'd like to stand on mimes.) The feeling I had in my dream was "Nope, I don't want to play." Life can be pretty isolating in the 21st century without connection and I think my dream was a reflection of modern life, 100 people leading separate lives together.

Isolation and loneliness are devastating.

It is the nature of someone discovering their creative side to get more in touch with their emotions, to try to express themselves and to even wonder where inspiration comes from. New artists have a huge advantage over experienced artists, they bring a curiosity and enthusiasm that eventually wears off, that's why experienced artists are always looking for new media and new inspiration, they want that freshness. While getting better technically is important, going through the motions will eventually kill you.

It isn't just experienced artists going through the motions.

I get a lot of letters (Ok, E Mails) from readers who are dealing with problems a lot deeper than I can share with you. They tell me that the Beast has offered them their first glimmer of hope in years, that beginning to look at life as an artist has made all the difference to them. Many of them are realizing that they aren't broken after all. Many of them find the connection and support of this new community to be their lifeline.

So; if your emotions are shut off, if you are feeling isolated, if you are on the verge of hopelessness, I get that. I have my moments too, moments when my day is nothing more than a to do list, when there is no hope of joy, days you just hope to get through. Days when I am overwhelmed, when doing anything besides playing solitaire on my computer requires too much effort. Isolation and loneliness are devastating, your only alternative is to get very numb.

When I feel that way, I sit down and write; maybe a piece like this. I look for laughter, I try to help someone else, I look for stars and angels, I listen for the voices of friends. I let my Beast out and then I begin to come back to life again. I hope you will do the same, and that we continue to help each other become the artists we truly are.

You are an artist. Artists emote.

Often, creativity comes in response to solving a problem or filling a need, sort of like solving a real cool puzzle. Other times, storytelling is an important component of creativity, how many times have you heard a song or looked at a painting that tells a story. The cool thing about mid life? We have lots of stories to tell. I mentioned the book The Shack, it shows that good stories, don't necessarily have to epic tales.

A good story, well told, can be about a simple little event that everyone can identify with, it's about conveying a message that helps people make major life decisions. Stories are how we teach, people make decisions about their own lives with the help of stories they have heard. The more your work teaches and gives someone a message, the more powerful and long lasting it will become.

Stories can come from books, form paintings, from movies, from songs. The most influential book in history? The Bible, it's a collection of stories. In his book Story, (the classic book on writing an effective screenplay) Robert McKee says people like stories because it helps them decide "What kind of life should I live?" You have stories to tell, so do I.

In fact; I'll tell you one: One beautiful spring day I was cruising the Banana River in my boat Amie. I had the boat up on plane, probably going 30 miles an hour and enjoying the wind whipping through my hair. I love my boat, I love being on the water and I spend as much time on them as I possibly can. Grace seems to live there.

The sun was up, it was one of those days where the river was so flat it looked like you were gliding across a painting, dolphins were playing nearby, aside from them and a few birds, we had the water to ourselves. All of a sudden, I heard a voice, I literally heard a voice, that said, "Shut it down." My journey through creativity has taught me nothing if it not to pay attention to voices: I shut the boat down. Just like that, the bow went back in the water and I was gently drifting in the Intracoastal Waterway.

The voice, who I've dubbed my Guardian Angel, said, "Not the boat, the Affluent Artist" (my last book).

"But that's my baby, I have plans for that book."

"I have something better, something that will help more people."

And on it went, me sitting there talking to an angel in the middle of a river while some must have wondered if I was catching the schizophrenia. Maybe I was. But within 2 days, I had trademarked Middle Aged Crazy and done all the other things that a writer does to begin a project.

My life has been richer and fuller since because of the wonderful people I talk to every day and the wonderful message of inspiration I received on the boat. Inspiration has not abandoned me after giving me the idea. I have been awakened in the middle of the night by my noisy angel, I have found myself writing at times when the words are coming through me, not from me and I have never, not even once, been at loss for things to write about. I have found my calling in life by listening to inspiration and by saying "Yes and..."

Chapter 7 Exercises

Artists emote. A great source of inspiration is the emotions you experience throughout your day. I'd like you to keep track of all the weather fronts of emotion that sweep through your day. Make a note of when you are happy, annoyed, frustrated or overwhelmed. Keeping in touch with your emotions will help you to harness then for creativity. Try it for a day and, if you like, continue for a week or so until you get used to it.

Keep an inspiration log. Note how many times you think of something that might be useful in your creative pursuit and then note if you dismissed it or said "Yes and…" The more you practice saying "Yes and" the more inspiration will show up.

What is flow like for you? Can you describe what it feels like to be channeling from a higher place? When you are really lost in your work, what's it like?

What is your ideal environment for getting in flow?

"Imagination is more important than knowledge. For knowledge is limited to all we now know and understand, while imagination embraces the entire world, and all there ever will be to know and understand."
Einstein

· 8 Getting Some Skills

Ray's Story: Well, I thought I'd pick up a guitar and music would come out. Eventually. Not really, I mean I couldn't hold the chords down, it took me forever to change from one chord to the next, it actually felt like my fingers was stuck to the fret board. And then rhythm? Not so much! It was embarrassing, I was taking lessons in between two kids who were in grammar school. My teacher taught me like I was going out for the school band, he wanted me to get ready for recital. "Excuse me?" I wasn't going to play "Twinkle, Twinkle Little Star" at a recital; that's not what I signed up for! Thankfully, I found another instructor who helped me learn at my pace, he's willing to teach me the songs I want to hear and he is very encouraging too. I really notice a big difference in my playing. Will I make a band someday? I don't know, it just makes me happy to make a little noise. With my amplifier, I can make a LOT of noise! Finding the right teacher has been very important part of my progress. I tried to teach myself, but I was getting no where.

Lynn's Story: I am a little slower at learning new techniques than I used to be. My girls seem to pick things up faster than I do, it's like I have to erase all the old habits before I can lean new ones. That's why I love Becky, she is a very patient teacher. We've become friends who paint together, rather than a student and a teacher. She shows me stuff as we paint and I always feel so happy after one of her classes. I know I am getting better at my painting, but that's not the point. I just really enjoy the time I spend painting, it's the highlight of my day. If I didn't improve I think I'd get bored. Becky seems to know when I need a little stimulation and when she has a teachable moment. I appreciate that.

So, you have listened to the voice of inspiration, found your emotion and you sit down at the piano, ready to proclaim your passion... Only... You can't play.

Sigh.

That's ok, you've decided to find a new medium of expression, Good for You! It's going to take a little work to get better. In the meantime, I highly recommend that you start to journal your feelings, getting tuned into emotion will help you as an artist. Even if your medium does not involve the written word, keeping a journal of things that might trigger your creativity is a terrific exercise. You'll start to understand what makes you tick, creatively and, perhaps, otherwise.

You'll be surprised how quickly you CAN express yourself creatively. Don't get too caught up in technique and getting it "right", technical skill is inevitable if you practice. The blues are built around three chords and Ernest Hemingway became a great writer by using, short, declarative sentences. Dave Matthews had a handful of songs to begin his career with. In the meantime, journaling about your emotions is a huge step towards getting in touch with the feelings you want to communicate.

All of this creative stuff doesn't work if you don't have an outlet, does it? How did we become so un-artistic, a nation of spectators? It's fashionable to blame everything on "the media" and, in this case, it's correct. We can have any kind of entertainment we desire by a simple mouse click. Without leaving the couch, we can hear the greatest singers, the best musicians, the funniest comedians. It's easy to take their talent and greatness for granted, easy until we are asked to perform ourselves!

In our Great Grandparents time, before radio, before mass media, almost every home had a musical instrument of some kind. The only way people heard music at home was if they made it. We didn't worry so much about quality as we worried about participation. People who couldn't sing told stories, all of history was "remembered" before it was "recorded". Naturally funny people were encouraged to brighten a room with their talent. And, we didn't have a great big measuring stick like the media to compare ourselves to. Can't sing like some guy on the radio? What's a radio? People appreciated the efforts anyone made to entertain them because life was... well, so damn boring!

That's flip flopped, we don't entertain anyone else, we are entertained. What would you do if a neighbor invited you over for a sing along? Been to a barn dance lately? Pumped the pedals on a player piano in the last few decades? Why would you, really?

Why listen to your neighbor try to sing when you can watch Glee on Hulu? Everything we do artistically is quietly measured against something from the media. Can I play the solo just like the record? Can I dance like John Travolta? Am I as funny as Conan O'Brien? People might have the good sense to compare you in front of them, but in the back of their mind, you know they are thinking, "He's pretty good, but he better keep his day job." (It's ok, keep the day job!)

We are really good at being entertained, not so good at doing the entertaining. Thanks to mass communications, the only musicians we hear are "amazing". In fact, most people will tell you, "I can't sing." Can you imagine a tribal dance where no one danced or sang? Studies have been done with isolated tribes, when people from our culture are imbedded with them, the tribal members literally do not understand the statement, "I don't sing".

That's what has happened to our tribe, we demand entertainment and aren't willing to give any back! Every culture has a tradition of ritual song and dance. Of course you can sing, you just can't sing well enough to sell a bunch of tickets, but you CAN sing. You can dance, you can paint, you can write. It's that invisible measuring stick that is holding you back, it's self editing.

Here are a few keys:

Be patient with yourself. The Creative Beast says, Allow Yourself to Suck." If you think about it, we put so much pressure on ourselves to do something perfectly, we often forget the joy of the journey, of learning a new creative skill. You don't have to be a famous creative, you just need to be creative. We are old enough to appreciate the journey, to find joy in what little progress we make. Besides, it will make our kids think we've gone crazy and that's a real good thing!

"Allow yourself to suck" is something I came up with when I took up guitar. After a life of athletics and business, I had bought into all that "Expect Excellence" stuff. I was expecting, it turns out, to be perfect at everything. I'd picked up a guitar with the intention of learning to play a few times during my life. And; each time, I'd set aside, I wasn't prepared for just how difficult it was for me to get sound out of my favorite instrument.

"I am going to master this no matter what," I said through gritted teeth. And I worked very hard at guitar, but I was having NO FUN. Finally, a guitar teacher looked at me, a little impatiently, and asked, "Why are you getting mad?" And, I started to go into this whole, "I expect excellence thing."

He just looked at me and said, "This is supposed to be fun."
He was, of course, right. Learning to play guitar is fun, I
appreciate every squeak, buzzed chord and un-rhythmic
sound that comes out of my instrument. Once I released
that "I want to master this damn thing" attitude and began
to enjoy it, I realized I had a hobby that would last me a
lifetime. One that I would never quite master and that's OK!
Do I play any songs that sound "just like the record?" Not
many, but that's ok too, I am making music and the fact
that the guitar is pressed right against my heart is not lost
on me. Playing guitar makes my soul happy.

Talent, by the way, has very little to do with success, when
it comes to creative pursuits. It turns out, it's the time you
put in. Now, because of positive feedback, we are more
likely to keep practicing something that comes easily to us,
but, even if you think you have no "talent" a good teacher
can help you overcome this hurdle. Talent, is way overrated.
If you find your "element" you will get good at it; at least
good enough to express yourself. I promise.

Successful creatives are amazingly disciplined people. The
guy you see on stage might make it look easy, but he's
probably trained his whole for the few minutes he gets to be
out there. Most people are fairly certain that they could be a
stand up comedian with a little practice and a few drinks. Try
it, I dare you. The guy who does 5 minutes on Letterman
has probably been honing that set for more than a decade.
Making something look easy is a talent all by itself.

My standard answer when someone asks if it is difficult to
write a book? "It's really easy, they give you all the letters,
you just have to rearrange them."

Like anything else you want to succeed at, getting better at your creative pursuit will require that you set some goals and develop a way to keep yourself accountable. Give yourself little rewards for hitting certain benchmarks as you gain more technical skill. But, I want you to remember something: Technical skill is fine, but your goal is to be an artist, not a technician. It's easy to get so caught up in learning your new craft that you forget to feel free enough in your medium to express yourself. You wouldn't be a very good writer if you focused on punctuation and capitalization only. No, a good writer communicates, the technical aspects of writing might make communicating easier, but punctuation is not a substitute for powerful prose.

A few years ago I was standing on the Santa Monica Pier doing a radio interview on my cell phone (now, that's a statement I never thought I'd make when I was a religious studies major trying to figure out how I'd ever gain employment) and I was asked this:

"What about the people who want to live the artist's lifestyle, that think it is all about partying, sleeping late and rocking out?"

What about them? They aren't artists, that's what. I've gotten to know hundreds of artists, professional and amateur (whatever that means) and I can tell you this: artists are disciplined. Even the burned out rocker has put in his time and developed his talent, otherwise, he'd have gone away. Slackers don't succeed for long at anything, especially something that requires creation.

I saw the Eagles not long ago in concert and if anyone lived the rock pharmacological lifestyle, it was them. And; if anyone could go through the motions on stage, it would be this Baby Boomer's favorite band (like we could hear the difference anyway!). And do you know what? They didn't. They hit every note, they brought feeling to their music, they even wore shined shoes. The Eagles did not mail it in.

When it comes to those of us who are new creatives, the lesson of the Eagles is important: artists are disciplined. If you decide to embark on a new creative pursuit, you need to schedule your creative time like anything else that is important to you: set goals and have some means to hold yourself accountable. If you don't, days and then weeks will go by and you'll find yourself saying: "I wonder what happened to that piece?"

Deciding to Release Your Beast only goes as far as the action you take. Buying the paintbrushes, the paint, the easel and the canvas doesn't make you an artist. Neither does wearing a smock around the house. I have a friend who has been a professional saxophone player for 30 years. He still takes lessons and practices everyday. The thing about art: it takes work. Hopefully, you love the work so much that you don't notice.

My suggestion: add "Create cool stuff" to your To Do List everyday, your whole day will be better. You'll spend the time before you create looking forward to creating, you'll be engaged while you create and you'll feel good about your creation when you are finished. When you close your eyes at night, you'll realize you spent the whole day thinking like an artist and that's a magnificent feeling.

If you want to get to a point with your creativity that you can adequately express yourself, you'll need to reach a certain level of competency, I mean, how boring would it be to play chopsticks all the time? Artists are a lot more disciplined than you might think. Setting aside to learn new skills and master old ones is part of this journey. Writers are readers too, musicians listen to other musicians and painters go to galleries. Taking a class, hiring a teacher and admiring the work of others is only useful if you are going to imprint the new techniques into your muscle memory and your brain. That takes practice.

The stereotype, in my case, is true: I'm enough of a guy to hate asking for directions. (That's the genius of GPS, by the way, some woman figured out if you create a shiny gadget men will enthusiastically ask for directions: and then argue with it.) Self teaching only goes so far, I've become an enthusiastic student on this journey through Middle Aged Crazy. When it comes to selecting a teacher to learn more about your creative outlet, I have some tips, some things I've learned the hard way.

Whether you are learning a new musical instrument, a new craft or any hobby, learning as an adult is different (for one thing, your parents aren't forcing you to take lessons!) Deciding which teacher will aid and abet the escape of your creative beast is a crucial decision. I've talked to several people who gave up on the process, not because they "weren't talented" but because someone who was a "teacher" said something to crush their confidence. Before you sign up for a class or hire an instructor, you need to ask these questions, signing up for any instruction without the right answers is done at the peril of losing your Beast.

1. *"Do you teach adults AND do you like teaching beginners?"* I took guitar lessons from a guy who taught kids, my lesson time at the music store was between a 9 year old and a 10 year old. I really wasn't interested in learning Mary Had a Little Lamb (And this guy never heard of Fire and Rain!) so we were a bad fit, I wasn't trying out for the school band and he thought the Beatles were a fad. Does your teacher know how to work with grown ups, people who will ask questions? Adults will take control of a lesson and not learn anything if the teacher doesn't know the different techniques required to teach adults. Also, does the teacher really love to teach or is he just some starving artist who decided teaching would be a good way to pick up a few bucks? You must find a teacher who loves to watch you progress. How do you find this out?

2. *"Can I Ask Lots of Questions"*, not just in the lessons, but before? Your instructor: Who has he taught, what does he teach, how does he feel about E Mail questions? You are an adult and YOU, not your parents, are paying for the lessons, make sure you are on the way to learning what you want to learn. It's up to you to set learning goals, before the class is chosen, before each class and for your homework between. Teachers can teach better if you have learning goals. I'm not suggesting you take over the class or make demands that are not within the course boundaries, but make sure that you are going to learn what you came to learn. Keep in mind, you might only be building the base to learn what you want to learn.

3. *"Is it a nurturing environment?"* Look, at this stage, you probably aren't going to make the Russian Ballet, so you don't need to hire a teacher who makes the learning process anything less than fun. Drill instructors, football coaches and Miss Arigi (my 5th grade English teacher) might get certain results by bullying people: don't hire them. (Lets remember that mindset: you ARE hiring them, you are the boss). You want someone who will allow you to ask questions, who understands that we might not have a lot of talent. In my case, I am slow to learn new guitar techniques. It takes me a few weeks to learn a song that some people can get in a few minutes. I'll get it eventually, it will simply take a while longer. If my teacher so much as made one disparaging remark, I'd be crushed. He doesn't; he gets it. Does your teacher expect you to get it at once or is he patient with you? Opt for patience. It only takes one ill timed remark to pound the Beast in the forehead.

4. *What is Your Best Learning Environment?* Are you better in a group? Can you learn from DVD's or do you need the individual feedback that comes with private lessons? Some people need a combination, like a group I know that buys a DVD and learns from it together. You may have to sample a few different methods to find your best way to learn, keep in mind, everyone is a little different. What works for others might not work for you and that's ok, the important thing is that you don't give up because of a bad fit.

5. *Is Your Teacher Enthusiastic?* Your teacher should love the subject at least as much, if not more, than you. A lack of talent can be eclipsed by an abundance of zeal. In my case, I have Improv teachers and a guitar instructor who are so turned on by their craft that it is infectious. In Improv, their enthusiasm has saved me several times from feeling overwhelmed and giving up. With guitar, my experience with bad teachers was only overcome by my passion for the instrument I love so much. Dave, my current teacher, loves guitar with every fiber of his being and it shows. Look your teacher in the eye and gauge his passion for the subject, if it isn't there, run!

When you reach the point where your Creative Beast needs a little help, be careful about who you select. The wrong instructor might make you feel inadequate and hopeless and the right one will help you become the artist you know you truly are!

We've reached a point in life where this new art form is something that is really, really meaningful to us and we really WANT to master it. So, understand that it's ok to not be very good at first and enjoy every little tiny piece of progress that you make. Before you know it, you'll be showing everyone what an artist you are.

Chapter 8 Exercises

How much time, a day, can you set aside to get better at your creative pursuit? Not the time you spend creating, but how much time can you spend solely with the intent of getting better?

Now is the time to write down your creative goals. What do you want to accomplish?

Lists Rock! This is a great time to get in the practice of making a daily list of at least 2 things to move you towards your creative goal: "Write a paragraph", "Research Cold Fusion", "Practice mime silently for 15 minutes". Get in the habit, before you go to bed, of writing your next day tasks. Let's start now:

We recommend an accountability partner. Your daily accountability calls are not social calls, they should last about 5 minutes: "Did you do what you said you were going to do?" "What are you going to do today?" Is pretty much the extent of the call, telling someone your plan for the day helps to lock it in.

-
-
-

9 Join a Tribe

Ray's Story: I found a place to jam. I can't believe I did it, in fact the first time I went, I left my guitar at home. It's this Friday night jam that's been meeting for years in a strip mall parking lot. They play bluegrass, which I don't even like, but that's ok, the jam is open to all and after checking it out, I started to show up: with my instrument. They play real simple stuff, usually the same three chords for every song, and it makes me feel like a real musician to be able to strum along. For now, I sit on the outside of the circle, strumming along to the rhythm. Some day I'll take a solo, but I'm not there yet! The cool thing is that I've made some friends and we chat about playing over the internet a couple of times a week. It helps me to set goals for my playing, I want to keep up with my friends!

Lynn's Story: So, I took this little corner of the condo and kind of walled it off with a room divider. It's near the window and the light is good. Funny thing, I had to rearrange almost the whole place to claim my little space, but I like it, I don't have that "I should be cleaning up the mess" thought on my mind as I paint. Here's the other thing, I have this baseball cap and when I wear it, the girls know they are only to come near me if the cat is in the deep fryer. When I wear the hat, I am officially not home and in art land. (I love it in art land). They seem ok with it, I guess I'm not bothering them either!

There's an old motivational poster that says, "It's tough to soar with the Eagles when you are surrounded by turkeys." Making a choice to live a more creative life requires that the people you see, the places you work and even the thoughts you think be designed to maximize your creative process. Your Creative Beast has a little ADD and is easily distracted. Bills, unfinished business, emotional issues and other distractions can send him back to his cave.

Creativity comes from being able to recognize and trust your creatives instinct. It's hard to do that if your mind is elsewhere. Actually, when I'm talking about environment, I'm talking about something called "de-cluttering". It's about your physical location, your relationships and your creative routine.

Let's talk about your creative environment. Creativity involves freeing your mind, releasing resistance and putting yourself in a position to follow your creative instincts. You can't do that if you have "clutter." Clutter takes a surprising amount of energy from you. Unfinished jobs, broken relationships and physical clutter are all things we call "incompletes," the more incompletes you have in your life, the less energy you have to be creative.

Clutter can be internal or external. Clutter can be a messy closet, each time you walk past it you spend a little energy saying, "I really should clean that someday." Clutter can be the distraction of other people talking to you when you are trying to create. It can be internal conflict that gets in the way of your inspiration. For example; dealing with loneliness and heartbreak might motivate you to do some of your best work if you can channel it... But if you can't, they become clutter... If you've just had a knockdown drag out with one of your kids, that "incomplete" might overpower your ability to create. While good art does comes from emotion, Clutter can overwhelm you and rob you of creative energy.

Your Creative Beast is a sensitive little guy, one who is easily distracted and overwhelmed. Strong emotions, unfinished business and other distractions give resistance a chance to sneak in and take you away from the important stuff. It's important that you find your own creative comfort zone, that you design an environment that gives you a chance to compete with resistance. How can you do this?

Most important, do the people in your life understand what you want to do creatively? Have you asked them for help? I suggest you call a family meeting and let them know the ground rules: "I need an hour a day to work on my project and I'd rather not be interrupted." or words to that effect will go a long way in letting them know how important this is to you. Sneaking around or hoping they'll figure it out will probably doom you to failure.

Here's a big thing to know: if they don't cooperate, you don't get to give up and play victim. Nope, it's not their responsibility to release your beast, it's yours and you'll just have to find time to do this important work for yourself. Get up earlier, work at your desk through lunch, turn off your favorite shows at night. Don't give up at this first sign of resistance.

In my experience, the people around you don't have to completely understand your creative urges to support you. It's perfectly ok to say, "I just need a little time for myself." Asking for permission gives away a lot of power; just make a statement instead. If they think you've gone a little crazy and need to go off to learn to play the triangle, let them think it. However, most of the people I've talked with are surprised at how much support and admiration they actually get from the people around them.

The advantages of getting the people in your life on board is pretty obvious, it would be great to have the people in your life there to support and encourage you. Learning a new creative outlet is quite an undertaking for an adult, asking for a little help, a little encouragement might be hard at first. Once your family sees your enthusiasm and your progress, they will rally behind you even more. Who knows? Some of them might decide to join you!

Have you given much thought to your physical environment? You know, a creative space? Everyone is a little bit different, but let me explain that you are looking for a physically functional space that will allow you to go deep into creative flow. If you can't get comfortable or can't work without interruption, you won't get as much done. You will, in fact, create less cool stuff.

Some artists I know are VERY picky. They need a clean desk, a certain pen, and perfect silence. Others only require a dark, quiet place. In my case, I need stimulus to write, I'm better with I Tunes on or even in a crowded Panera's than in solitude. (That's is, when I am finally writing. When I am deciding what to write, I need a hot shower or a quiet place). If I have a noise, like music, to distract MOST of my brain, the writing part can really flow. If its too quiet, the other parts of my brain get distracted by shiny stuff.

You might need a certain type of chair, a room with a lock on the door or a space over the garage; the important thing is that you understand that your environment must be conducive to your particular creative outlet, you might need to try a few different arrangements. Once you find one that works for you, flow will come more easily.

Your creative time is not going to happen if you don't plan it into your day. Whether you need to write it in your calendar or just have a set time everyday for your creative pursuit, I believe, strongly, that if you don't plan on it, you won't get around to it. If you don't plan it, the next thing you know, a week has gone by and then a few weeks and... before you know it, you are wondering about what ever happened to your creative project. I mentioned the War of Art before, and its author Steven Pressfield says he will sit in front of his computer and stare at it for 2 hours everyday, even if he thinks he has nothing to say. The discipline of following a routine helps creative flow to show up.

Removing physical clutter from your life will make you more creative, at least that is my experience. Cleaning the attic might not seem like a direct result to being a better painter, but you'd surprised at how much energy we spend on "incompletes" and "Some days." We only have so much energy, why not have all of it available for your art?

Physical clutter can give resistance just enough of a hole to crawl through to take you off your game. Listen to yourself the next time you walk by that messy room or closet. "Someday, I really ought to clean that up," and then you feel a little guilty. The next thing you know, you can't come up with the right metaphor for your story because you are thinking about how your Dad used to yell at you for having a messy closet. (I hate when that happens.)

Stuff in the back of your mind can get VERY loud and really drain your energy. Doubt that? Go clean that closet and see how good you feel the next time you stroll by it! Unfinished business, or "incompletes" are issues that come up in the middle of our creative time, before you know it, our mind can be thinking about how much our sister pisses us off or how you wish you hadn't been so unkind to your spouse. Creativity works better when you are present and resolving the clutter of personal incompletes has many good consequences, not the least of which is it will make your soul happier.

The word discipline sends chills down your spine, it conjures images of Nuns slapping your bare hand with rulers, drill sergeants screaming in your face or being told to wear a dunce cap and stand in the corner. We live in fear of being disciplined.
Words morph, they take on a new meaning over time, my kids' favorite adjective is "amazing", I tease them that they are easily amazed. To them, amazing is simply a term of approval and mild wonder, like, "This celery juice is AMAZING!" My generation isn't immune, we adopted the word "Cool", a more subdued form of amazement. "Dad, don't you think this celery juice is AMAZING?" "Yeah, it's cool."

I looked up the word "Discipline" and its Latin roots are from the words "instruction and knowledge", like Christ's Disciples. Not exactly the first image we think of when we are being disciplined! I'm talking about discipline today because it has been coming up in my life lately. In an interview I did with author Peter Clothier, he mentioned that the importance of his daily yoga and meditation was the "discipline". The act of sitting down and taking time out of his day, every day, lends structure to his life. On my faith journey, many years ago, I read a book called, Celebration of Discipline and in fact, the Methodist "owners manual" is called, The Book of Discipline.

Not long ago; I decided to incorporate good diet and meditation into my day as well and I realized, after talking to Peter, that I have been living a fairly disciplined life. Imagine that! Me! This "self discipline" is leading to more knowledge about my well being and I haven't hit my bare hand with a ruler, even once. The concept of having a daily "practice" is appealing to me, and it isn't about discipline in the way we usually use the word: I do it because I want to, not because I face a punishment if I don't.

If you talk to successful artists, as I have, you'll come to respect their discipline to their craft, not that they could help it! When you find your "element" (your passion), you can't help but get better at it, it consumes you. In the book Outliers, Malcolm Gladwell explained to us that it takes 10,000 hours to truly master something and that's a big problem with finding your creative outlet later in life: TIME.

Sure, maybe learning to play oboe is on your bucket list, but when are supposed to find *one* hour, never mind 10,000? You imagine yourself picking up you oboe, making squeaking sounds for 20 minutes or so and then what? You aren't playing like the great oboe masters, in fact, you are no different than the 5th grader who picked it up for the first time. (You suck.) It's no fun to suck, especially at something frivolous, like playing a musical instrument. You have better things to do.

You don't.

It isn't frivolous. And: if you allow yourself to suck it IS fun. Get over that 10,000 hour thing, you probably aren't going to master the oboe, at least not for quite a while. But; you will see progress. Your oboe muscles will get bigger, you'll get stronger, you'll see progress. And seeing progress is an important motivational factor in anything we do. If you can find something that fascinates you and see just a little improvement, you'll be hooked, maybe for life. Before you know it, you'll be bringing your oboe to parties, planning oboe cruises and listening to the all oboe channel on satellite radio.

Talented people who don't have discipline are no different than non talented people without it. Talent is a great place to begin, but not a requirement to find your creative outlet. Just because something comes easily to you, it doesn't mean it will be your passion. Often, something that challenges us is just what we are looking for.

If you find a creative outlet that grabs a hold of you, you WILL find the time to do it. Maybe a little less television, maybe a little less Facebook, but you'll find the time. No one will have to force you, no Nuns will threaten you with a ruler. I've done it and you can too. Just give yourself permission and you'll soon be amazing yourself at how "disciplined" you can become. Having a creative passion makes everything better.

How cool is that?

Here's another idea about your surroundings, join a tribe! Finding others to work with, other people who will share your journey is an important part of your success. It would be wonderful if you could find a mentor, someone who is just a little ahead of you on the journey. Here's the main reason people don't have mentors:

They don't ask.

Imagine if someone came up to you and said, "I love your work, could you help me?" Wouldn't you be inclined to say yes? Some of the most successful people I know have volunteered to mentor someone, just because they asked! The right mentor can save a lot of time, can help you avoid the big mistakes and give you the encouragement you need.

I am a big believer in having an accountability partner and a mastermind group. If you can find people who share your drive and interest and are willing to help you stay committed to success, you will find that your task gets easier, nobody wants to be a Lone Ranger. Success is a team sport and, as tempting as it is for artistic types to be lone wolves, it's better to work with the support of a Mastermind Group and a good accountability partner.

An accountability partner is simply someone you speak with everyday, in my case, I talk in the morning with mine. An accountability call takes no more than 5 minutes, if done right. You simple say what you did the day before and what you plan o do that day. It's that simple. No excuses, no long conversations. Then your partner tells you. The very act of telling someone what you plan to do sets your plan in motion. A good accountability partner will learn to recognize your excuses and will force you to "play up."

A mastermind group is along the same idea, only they meet weekly or every two weeks. I've seen some that meet locally for coffee and others, like mine, who meet electronically (we use Skype). The Mastermind Formula, is for a group of no more than 6 or 8 to meet to discuss goals, ask for help and make commitments before the next meeting. You offer advice, make introductions and again, hold each other accountable. The meetings are held to a strict 1 hour time limit and a timekeeper is appointed for each meeting.

If you can form a mastermind group of other creatives, even if you don't all work in the same discipline, you will be amazed at the progress you will achieve by working with other goal oriented people. My group includes people from all over the United Sates, the Caribbean and London, we are all entrepreneurs from a variety of businesses and it is a powerful way to spend an hour every two weeks. I am charged up after every call.

There is a school of thought that says you become the 5 people you spend the most time with. By putting yourself in the right environment, you will become more creative. By finding a tribe of people, either on line or virtually who share your goals, you will find that the journey gets easier.

Chapter 9 Exercises

How much time, a day, can you set aside to get better at your creative pursuit? Not the time you spend creating, but how much time can you spend solely with the intent of getting better?

Now is the time to write down your creative goals. What do you want to accomplish?

Lists Rock! This is a great time to get in the practice of making a daily list of at least 2 things to move you towards your creative goal: "Write a paragraph", "Research Cold Fusion", "Practice mime silently for 15 minutes". Get in the habit, before you go to bed, of writing your next day tasks. Let's start now:

We recommend an accountability partner. Your daily accountability calls are not social calls, they should last about 5 minutes: "Did you do what you said you were going to do?" "What are you going to do today?" Is pretty much the extent of the call, telling someone your plan for the day helps to lock it in.

Seek not outside yourself, for all
your pain comes simply from a futile
search for what you want, insisting
where it must be found.
A Course in Miracles

· 10 What Happens at Mid Life?

Ray's Story: I've got to tell you, I am better at everything, including my job, since I Released My Beast. It's like I am more, I don't know, engaged in my own life. I have more energy, more enthusiasm. I mean, it's stupid to say strumming a few guitar chords and writing a blog would change me, but it has! I have more to talk to people about, more things that interest me. Who'd have thought one of my best clients was in a rock band? Now we have lunch and talk about music, we just do business over desert! So, yes, if you think I am happier now, you'd be right. All that rage, that frustration is mostly gone, I can rip off a good blog post about the anger that stays with me and I feel better about it.

Lynn's Story: I always knew I was an artist, that I'm painting now is not a great surprise. What is a surprise is how long I didn't paint. I had a life to live, kids to raise and I wouldn't trade my journey for anyone's. Now I have learned so much, I have so much to share with others. Through my art, I am already helping my daughter and there will be many other kids I can help. My Mother would be proud.

"This is a great class, you guys are funny, you are really good at listening and supporting each other, but we have to do some exercises to ramp up the energy level. You are a very laid back class." Charles, our little Improv teacher, was trying to get us out of our adult shells, to "play bigger."

I have to tell you, writer guy here prides himself on being James Bond cool, on being able to slip into a room like a Ninja. Even in a raucous party, I am a shadow. Like a diver entering a pool with no splash, I can enter a room full of people without anyone knowing I was there and then write about it like I was the life of the party. There's quiet and then there's Me; quiet wonders when I am going to perk up a little.

So that's why I thought Charles was looking right at me when it came to the energy exercise. I'm pretty sure he knew, in the first week, I was uncomfortable simply standing on the stage of the empty theater and I slowly stretched each week. This night was the big stretch for me, being funny wasn't enough, I had to act enthusiastic, silly, and loud. I wasn't sure I had it in my DNA.

Here was the game, the sixteen of us formed a semi circle and Charles and the first volunteer did a little 10 second scene about a big brother and a little brother rolling marbles. Then, one player from each side of the semi circle would step in and replay the same scene, only bigger. Each pair after had to get even bigger, more emotion, more gestures, more over the top. Well, guess who was last? Yup, writer guy, and I found myself channeling Bruce Springsteen, oh yea, I was over the top! Not having ever been to the top of the experts slope before; I had no point of reference, I pointed the skis straight down the double X trail and got in a tuck.

If, like me, you have never, ever, gone over the top, I recommend it. I abandoned coolness, I was The Boss as a marble roller, I was... not me.

"Do you feel it little brother? Do you FEEEEEEEL It?"

And: the roof didn't fall in and people were laughing, laughing hard, and I didn't shrivel up and die. It was a Middle Aged Crazy moment at its finest, I stretched, I grew, and I only feel a little stupid telling you about it now.

Charles pointed something out, actually it was the point of the exercise: our Improv got a LOT better. Once we boosted the energy level up to a 10, we stopped filtering our scenes and just went with it, which is the whole point of Improv. Improv is about working together, as a team, to build a scene and see if something funny happens. That funny is more likely to occur if you go with your first impulse and don't try to force in something you were thinking before the scene started.

I'm pretty sure that raising the energy level, magnifying the emotion you are trying to communicate, will work in any creative outlet. This is probably why we think of artists as being a little eccentric. Being able to throw yourself totally into joy (or the blues, or jealousy, or love) leads to more spontaneous and deeper work. Granted, you have to achieve a certain skill level to produce good work, but, after channeling Bruce Springsteen, I believe that if you give two artists of equal talent the same project, the one who is more emotionally invested will produce better work.

The whole point of finding creativity in mid life is to give voice to your emotions. How about you, can you play bigger? Everyone, at some point in their life has either heard or used the phrase, "Living life to its fullest." It seems to imply that we should all be jumping off garage roofs into swimming pools filled with beer and naked people.

In reality, for most of us, living life to the fullest is not about thrill seeking or hedonism. I mean, they are worth a shot for some, but really, what does living life to the fullest mean to YOU? Because my answer is going to be different than yours, that's the fun of the journey.

Sometimes, we start out on a path and make the best decisions we can along the way only to find we weren't in charge of all the events in our lives. Some of us, who made all the right decisions still find ourselves with a lot of questions.

It's quite possible to come to a realization that we are not our possessions, not our titles, not out appointed roles. We came here, to existence, for something. Only, we get busy and forget what that something is.

We can't hide from it forever, our soul will find a way to get our attention. Call it your "Dharma", your "Destiny", your "Reason for Being". I'll call it "Meaning." It's looking for us.

Wayne Dyer's explanation of what happens to us as we go through some of the changes that are a normal part of reaching maturity. Dyer, in his book (and movie) The Shift, explains that we shift from an ego based motivation (ambition) to a life that requires us to search for meaning. It's natural to ask "Why did God make me?" and Dyer gives some pretty good clues to help discover own mystery of existence. It turns out, there are even differences between the way Men and Women approach this Shift.

Dyer recommends a book by William R. Miller and Janet C'de Baca called Quantum Change, a shift in which they describe an important change in the way mature adults approach life: a "vivid, surprising, benevolent and enduring transformation." Often, this change "Turns our value system upside down," and, in their study, the authors found some common changes that many of us experience. If you've been wondering what the heck is going on in your life; you aren't the only one wondering about what happens to us at mid-life! There is some pretty heavy change going on.

Men, who are still raised to be the hunter/gatherer in our society have these pre- Shift values:

"Wealth, Adventure, Achievement, Pleasure and Being Respected."

Sound familiar? Big job, big car, big adventures, big... You get the idea. We are encouraged to be ambitious, to have nice toys, moose heads on the walls, trophies, cigars... We're Men!

Women, before the Shift, are the nurturers, they value: "Family", yet there is a built in conflict, the next values are "Independence, Career, Fitting In and Appearance."

On my FB fan page, I asked what values had shifted among my readers and it is amazing how close the responses from women were to these. It is, in many ways, a lot easier to be a man! Women are expected to nurture, get along and look beautiful while being fabulously independent and successful. Can you do all that? (I can't.)

So, what happens? Why do we change? Sometimes it is the Biblical bolt of lightening that knocks us off the horse, sometimes it is more subtle. No matter, the period I've so ineloquently dubbed "Middle Aged Crazy" is about this quantum change, it's about this Shift.

We change.

In their study, Miller and C'de Baca found the "Post Quantum Change" values truly change our entire outlook on life. Men, for example, now value:

"Spirituality, Personal Peace, Family, God's Will, and Honesty." (

Not a red sports car in the bunch, is there?) Women, shifted to

"Personal Growth, Self Esteem, Spirituality, Happiness and Generosity." (So much for fashion!)

Going through life's passages and finding true meaning in our life is not something to be taken lightly. It can be painful to find that the path we started on is no longer the path we are supposed to be on. One might wonder if one's entire life, so far, has been a false start, have we been chasing the wrong things?

Usually, the answer is, "Not Really." We have all made the best decisions we could, we have all done the best we could. Facing the new challenges life presents to you, deciding not to "die with your music inside of you " (Dyer) might call for mid course corrections, but don't forget to place a high value on the road you have already traveled.

The people you love, the experiences you've had, the values that have guided you, have gotten you this far, take a minute and value them.

Mid life is not a number, not an age, and its a little bit of a moving target, we aren't ever really sure if we have reached our mid point in life. In a nutshell, midlife is a period when we have some time to look back and evaluate our history of making decisions. Like a football coach making halftime adjustments, we reach a point in life where we say,

"How did I end up here and where do I want to go now?"

It's a time when we begin to wonder what happened to our childhood dreams and try to remember why our soul came here in the first place. We often want very different things in the second half of life than we did in the first half. We want more meaning, we want to leave a legacy, we want to reconnect with our dreams, we want to accomplish something while we still have time. (Keep in mind, in 1900, average life expectancy was 45 years old, survival was the main focus of humanity. Today, we have the expected life span to ponder the reason for our own being.)

For many, this mid course adjustment is triggered by the end of a relationship, the loss of a job or our last kid going off to college. Sometimes it is just a feeling that we have been serving everyone else and it is time to serve ourselves, a feeling that we have made good decisions, yet still ended up in the wrong place. For some, these questions can be met with depression, avoidance or denial. Ignoring our souls is perilous business.

My research has led me to James Hollis PHD and his wonderful book, "Finding Meaning in the Second Half of Life, How to Finally Grow Up." Hollis is a Jungian psychologist, he believes that we have led our lives, initially, according to scripts handed to us genetically, by our parents and our environment. Only when we face our life choices and begin to acquire "real wisdom" do we find our "soul"; our authentic self (the root of the word psychology, "psyche", from the Greeks, is "soul", interesting how modern psychology won't ever use the term soul!)

Like Rick Warren's Purpose Driven Life, Hollis says "meaning" is trying to find us, not vice versa. Letting meaning find us is about letting go of "ego" and listening carefully to your soul, to the "real" reason you are here. The mission of the second half of life is to find out what is true for you. For you, not anyone else, you need to be setting off in the forest on your own.

As children we are helpless and dependent, we learn to survive by developing coping skills that often determine the way we relate to the world the rest of our lives. (For example: Fearful we are going to be left alone, we learn to please others etc.) It is only after recognizing our own patterns are we ready to grow, to find our true mission in life. "What summons me?"

Rediscovering your child like curiosity, your creativity, is just one vehicle to help you find meaning in your life. Hollis believes happiness is not our primary goal in life, finding meaning is.

No one else has taken your journey, no one else can sing your song. I hope you let us hear it! Because that is truly what "living life large" entails. Living life large is about the life you create, do you decide to play bigger or just read the script you were handed?

Creativity is a natural gift given to the created. Creativity is a sign of life, of growth, it's hard to stay alive if you aren't growing. Are artists happier people? No, like I've said, buying a box of crayons and a sketch pad won't solve all of your problems. But, approaching life with an artistic viewpoint will make it more interesting. Boredom is no fun.

Artists see scenes everywhere, musicians hear music on the subway, writers hear dialogue, in short, you are more in touch with your senses; more sensual. That can't be a bad thing. Artists appreciate contrast, they have a connection to life; they are bodies in motion.

So much of life is about momentum. Isaac Newton told us that resting bodies tend to stay at rest and a body will change its velocity only when an outside force is applied.

My list is my outside force.

"Drive", is a new book by one of my favorite authors, Daniel Pink. He talks about what motivates us, why we get our bodies in motion. He's mostly writing to the corporate market, telling employers that the old "carrot and stick" method of motivation works well with factory like, repetitive tasks but is actually counterproductive to "new economy" type creative jobs. His work applies to us on a personal level too, especially when it comes to finding our passions in mid life.

Give your kid a dollar every time he reads a book and he'll make the not too far leap that reading is work, something you only do if your parents bribe you. He'll lump reading in with taking out the trash and cleaning his room and totally miss the joy. Psychologists all over the world have tested the concept of paying bonuses and commissions and guess what? People cheat, they do just enough to make the goal, they bring less passion and artistry to their work.

So does that mean goals are bad? On the contrary, the only way I can get *anything* done is by setting them. Pink explains that there are three reasons we get our bodies in motion, I've alluded to them already:

Autonomy, Mastery and Purpose.

Autonomy means we are the masters of our own fate, my employer might pay me for my time, but I have not sold him my soul. I choose to do the work, I am the only one in control of me. Give me some freedom and you might find that I can do the job better than my boss thought possible. Give me robot like tasks and I will perform like one.

Mastery is about doing something because you want to "solve it", because it fascinates you, it's something you are not able to stop thinking about. That's why so many of us want to learn to play an instrument, take dance lessons or learn a language. We have a need to be challenged but we also want to see some progress. Jobs, of course, are better when we are fascinated by them. So is life.

Purpose is your raison d'etate, our purpose for being. Thinking we are "making a difference", "leaving a legacy" or "in our element" are more powerful than any bonus. Ask a schoolteacher or a triathlete. Ask the Sea Shepherds on Whale Wars. Someone "with a purpose" is a force not to be messed with.

I am often mocked, to my face, for having a "list" and I don't really care. When I am in achievement mode, I set 5 tasks a day, 5 things towards my goals that I do, even if I don't go to bed. I can often have five things done by lunchtime, sometimes it takes all day. My goal setting, which I learned in my year working with author and expert Jack Canfield, is about creating the momentum to achieve things most people would never attempt. Momentum is what happens when you are on task, working with a purpose. Unrelated things seem to appear when you have momentum, things that aren't even on your list.

My list is things I can do, not things that are dependent on someone else or other things I can't control. And, I release the outcome, if I work out every day, for 90 days and eat right, I should lose weight and inches, but I don't know how much. If I read 2 books a week and blog about them while talking to people about Middle Aged Crazy, I should be ready to write my book after 90 days. I don't have the control over whether it will be a NY Times bestseller.

If I practice my guitar ever day, I should get a lot better, but I can't control if I am ready to play on stage with Bruce Springsteen (But I can shoot marbles with him.) I focus on the tasks and let the journey unfold. Sitting on the couch will get me no where, so I vote for creating juice, momentum.

So much of life is about getting off the couch, about pushing yourself, about finding something that engages your passions. Do it one task at a time. I can't make all the right decisions about my diet, but I can make the NEXT right decision about it.

I hope you push play today!

Chapter 10 Exercises

Just for today, write down all of your inspirations. What ideas do you have for creativity? When the phone rings, do you know who it is before you look at caller ID? What did you get "right" today?

Story Starters:
Write the first sentence to 10 events in your life that you'd like to tell someone about. Think of events that have a lot of emotion associated with them.

1.

2.

3.

4.

5.

6.

7.

8.

9.

10.

Now, I think this goes a long way to your first 10 works of art. Even if you are building a piece of furniture or knitting a scarf, giving you piece a story changes your relationship with it.

All the world's a stage, and all the men and women merely players: they have their exits and their entrances; and one man in his time plays many parts, his acts being seven ages.
William Shakespeare

11 What Happens Now?

Ray's Story: You know, I always had to be right about everything. The words "I don't know" didn't exist in my world, I was expected to have the answers to everything. I was a business expert, a parenting expert, heck I even knew how to coach basketball better than the pro coaches. I had an opinion! The funny thing about learning some new creative stuff? I'm more interested in learning the things I don't know than in regurgitating what I do know. It's funny, but learning to be more creative has given me more energy to learn and stretch. I think I'm a lot more interesting person than I used to be. My advice? I wasted so much time when I could have been writing. Don't!"

Lynn's Story: I've spent too much time not painting, too much time wanting to be an artist. Funny thing, I was one all along. It's not my kids' fault, my ex-husband's fault or even my Mother's fault. It is actually no one's fault, I started to paint again wen I was ready to paint again. It's that simple. No bolt of lightening, no winning lottery ticket. One day, I just cleaned out a corner of the house and started to paint. My advice to anyone who asks? Just release the outcome and go for it! If you start to think like an artist, you will become one!

The ego is an amazing thing. Its job is to protect us, to keep us from failing, to let us know that we are, indeed, the center of the universe. Ego tells us we are separate individuals, we are born alone, we die alone. Ego can help us create, it's proud when we demonstrate our genius, when we show how talented we are. Creation that comes from ego is proud. Many artists create from ego. There is really nothing wrong with creating from ego.

Ego based creation does have a downside. It doesn't like the idea of us failing. It doesn't like the idea that creative genius might come from somewhere outside of us. It doesn't like it when we are new at something, not very good at something. Ego comes from lack; it tells us to Shame, Blame and Justify.

"I would really be terrible at the oboe." (Shame)

"I guess my parents should have sent me to oboe class." (Blame)

"So, I'll just let MY kids learn an instrument, it's too late for me." (Justify)

Have you listened to many ego based conversations like this? Shame, Blame and Justify is our egos way of deflecting responsibility, of protecting us, of convincing us that we are limited and should be comfortable with our limits.

The ego likes to worry about things like tomorrow, yesterday, grudges, insults and pain. Its job is to protect you, to insulate you from anything that might show you are not the powerful center of the universe. Ego worries about lack.

Creation, on the other hand, comes from abundance, not lack. As I explained earlier, artists usually feel like they are plugging
into the abundance of creation, into an unlimited source of creativity. By definition, the ego doesn't like the concept of ideas coming from outside of us, how can we be the center of the universe if we have to tap into a source beyond ourselves?

Many artists have HUGE egos, I'm not denying that. Putting yourself and your work "out there" is difficult and requires a pretty healthy self image. What I'm saying is, if you don't have the confidence, the training and the experience to be a new artist, your ego will try to talk you out of trying to become one. Resistance, the enemy, knows how to turn our own ego against us.

New artists, at middle age, have a special circumstance. You already have a fully developed ego, one that has a wholly developed defense system. Your biggest hindrance in Letting You be You?

Sorry to tell you: it's you. Actually, it's that evil S.O.B., resistance, using your ego to keep you from entering the loving world of creativity. I'll save your ego some trouble, each of them are excuses I've heard from my own Critters:

1. Who has time to learn a hobby?

2. I have no talent? It's too hard.

3. I don't know what to do.

4. I'm not creative.

5. I'm too old.

6. When I finish _____

7. My spouse would laugh at me.

8. I can't afford to.

9. I think I'll just sit here and watch TV

10. Guys (women) don't do that sort of thing

You can continue the list for as long as you like, what the heck, there is always a reason to do nothing. The status quo is probably just fine, isn't it?

Didn't think so.

Your creative side can save you. If you have a great job, being more creative will make it better. If you have the world's crappiest job, releasing your creative beast will make it tolerable. Why? Because the job will become a means to end, the source of funding for your materials, the place you get inspiration, the thing you do until you have time to play again.

So, what now? What's holding you back? Are you in overwhelm, are you afraid to get it wrong, are you unsure of your creative outlet? Hopefully, if you've read this far, you can release the excuses, you can move toward your dream, whatever it is.

In my journey though Middle Aged Crazy I've heard hundreds of stories of people whose lives (or sanity) has been saved by being creative in mid-life. Without exception, they are people who had other careers and decided to release their Creative Beast later in life. (An upcoming book will feature these stories).

I've talked with people who've fought illness and depression with painting. Women who have written plays that have been produced by local theater companies. Mom's who have been abandoned and carry on, singing with a band to keep themselves creative. Every so often I hear from someone whose spouse is terminally ill and the act of creating gives them the strength to carry on.

It's not just people who find a hobby who keep their soul happy. It's people who find a way to bring artistry and creativity to their "day job". The yoga instructor who uses her computer skills to build a successful practice. The Pastor's wife who uses art in her ministry, the science teacher who creates "Explosions" to teach science theory that kids will never forget.

Approaching life with your Creative Beast at you side makes every day an adventure. Obstacles become speed bumps and inspirations. People who bring their creativity to work excel, when we give an artist money to play with, we call him something different all together. We call him an entrepreneur.

Bringing the Beast to work is a good thing, it gives you a different view of ordinary tasks, it helps you to see the big picture. Artists are empathetic, so are good sales people. Artists see both sides of a problem, so do good negotiators. Artists create, so de business owners.

The reason we think of so many good artists as tortured souls is because they are. If you remove passion from your work, you are a technician. If a craftsman adds passion, adds his own little twist, he's an artist. I think it is that simple.

That's why a well respected business guru like Seth Godin has been screaming from the pulpit that business needs more artists. In a day when employees are supposed to work to their job description, read customer service scripts and do just enough to get by, the company run by artists will win.

When you have the right creative outlet, it will posses you. You'll start thinking about what to create in the shower. Then you'll process on it until you get to your creative area. As you create, you'll be so in flow that your time will fly, you are in the zone. After you create, you review you piece over and over, with some pride, with some eye for improvement. When you go to bed that night, you'll dream about your creation.

That's nice. You are an artist, at least you are thinking like one. You'll learn to draw on emotions instead of letting them control you, you will be more effective at everything. Anger, love, jealousy, joy: save those feelings, you'll need them to create. In the meantime, stay present. Present is good; especially at work.

Now, even if your day job is not about your art, you can't help but bring creativity to your work. It's coursing through your veins.

Why could being creative help save your life? Because it might. It's that simple.

Your feelings are the window to your heart. We can get pretty good at ignoring them, at tamping them down under daily tasks, hiding them behind actions for others, medicating them behind the mask of alcohol and television reality shows.

Once you begin to see your feelings as colors on your palette, you begin to handle them with a little more care; you pay a little more attention to them. Let's say you get angry with one of your kids. In mid bellow, "Because I said so…" You realize, "hey I need to use this later!"

It's been my experience that as you become more of an observer of your feelings, you find your self staying present longer and isn't that very Zen like? Controlling emotions is a bigger job for some of us than others, your author can use all the help he can get! By using your artist muscles to observe the world around you'll find that you are approaching life just a little differently. "How can I use this?" becomes your mantra and suddenly, inspiration is everywhere.

I've always been a fan of unflappable, quiet, confidant types. Probably because I have always been, well, flappable. Being the Master of your Domain is hard work. When you are always in survival mode, it's tough to enjoy life. In the last few years, I've tried to come from abundance, not from lack and it is better; it's easier to enjoy life when you aren't worried about everything that can go wrong.

Perhaps it's one of the benefits of aging, I now like to look at the bigger picture. I'm much more willing to release the outcome, to "allow" and that's something that astounds those who know me. As an aggressive, take charge, kind of guy, I built a career by shear will power and desire. I had the required focus and determination, an iron will. I had no time or patience for people who were slowing me down.

Something has changed. I hate to chalk it up to maturity, because I've always been "mature", hell, even when I was 8. (If anything, I've learned to be a little less boring lately.) No, this is a sea change, I noticed it when my daughter had a reaction to me last week that showed she was anticipating the "old" me. She got all defensive and went on a pre-emptive attack; one I would have deserved not long ago. It wasn't either one of our prouder moments; I realized I had taught her well.

See, the hardest prayer in the world for me has always been, "Thy will be done." In my opinion, I was given a life to create and charge after; it would be irresponsible to not become everything I could be. To say I was driven would be an understatement. (I think, because at heart I am not really a "Type A" personality). I played the role with such conviction that I was over the top. I wasn't happy with creating my own destiny, I also wanted to help everyone else along the way, I could be a little overbearing. Think of the financial guy with the red tie, 50 pounds overweight and with the heart condition. "Hard charging" would be a great way to put it and, being in a sales oriented career, I could do it with some polish, I am fairly persuasive.

It's easy to be reinforced in that role, the money is good, management loves you, your peers fear you. My Dad was hard charging and I was just like him. Only, Dad has really mellowed out. Eight bypasses will get your attention. Mine too. Chasing the money is over rated.

"Don't ask what the world needs. Ask what makes you come alive, and go do it. Because what the world needs is people who have come alive." Howard Thurman

137

Funny thing is, releasing my Creative Beast has been a huge difference, as I view life as more of an artist, I have become more of an observer. I'm learning to understand both sides of an argument, I'm learning, in short, to release.

I've been noticing that I am not as in control as I thought; have you experienced something similar?

I liked the ideas in The Secret: "you get what you attract" and Man; I was going to attract riches. We figured out, however, there is more to it than simply being determined. Did we attract this economy? Do people attract their own murder? Do we control things with our thoughts? No, we don't. All we can do is the best we can do, the rest is beyond our control. The "secret" of The Secret is in your own attitude, if you expect the best, you will recognize it when it comes along.

It's not popular to admit, but I am still a huge Tiger Woods fan. He lives in my town and is going through some self inflicted hard times. What drew me to him was his tenacity, I swear, I thought he used to be able to will the golf ball into the hole. Single minded, it turns out, has its dark side and Tiger has been re-examining his behavior too. The other day he said that he doesn't play with the same intensity that he used to, of his troubles he said, "It forced me to look deeper into myself and … how I grew up and how those things didn't match with the person who I am, and getting back to that, getting back to how my parents raised me. It's been good. I'm very excited about the future because of that."

I feel the same way, that I want to get back to who I am. I've had to learn to "release" that I am not responsible for someone else's actions, that I can only put my intentions out there and work towards them. I've had to learn that the world won't end if every decision doesn't go my way. I've learned that my ego is not always my best asset. (It hates this paragraph).

Recently, I've had some personal issues, some things have happened which I realized I had no control over. It's reinforced to me that staying present, in the now, is the only sane response to the world. Does that mean I sit back and do nothing, become a spectator to my own life?

No.

I still am driven, still set goals, but I am much more willing to release the outcome. I can still make my list, but I don't have to threaten slow or painful deaths to anyone who gets in the way. I can only control what I can control.

At basketball games in the last few years, I have been practicing observation and staying present. I watch my fellow season ticket holders bellow at the referees, chide the coach and question the players. While I want my beloved Orlando Magic to win, I realize the referees don't really care what I think of their calls. All I can do is observe, root and send my energy to the good guys. The rest is up to them. I am still engaged in the game, I simply realize that my ego is not a participant. The ego would have me stand up and point at the referees and scream at them until I am on the Jumbotron, "My opinion of you is indeed your business! I think you are making bad calls and you need to know that!" No they don't.

What happens when you ease back on the ego throttle? You begin to look at what matters, what's in the big picture.

I think finding your passion is the key to leading a happier life. I think unlocking your own creativity is the shortest route to that outcome. Plugging into your own version of genius turns into a fascinating way to go through the day. Little things don't bother you as much if you are more fascinated with creating cool stuff; if you are engaged in your own life. I don't know if this resonates with you, you might have figured this stuff out a long time ago. I have been known to be a slow learner. I do know this, looking at life through the eyes of a creative person has led to days that come with their own soundtracks.

I hope you dance! Because once you release that ego, you start to turn into some pretty powerful tools, things that have been there right along, you're just going to learn to major in them! I've come up with 7 things you can focus on:

PLAY: You remember how to play don't you? Recently, my daughter rescued a puppy from a puppy mill. This poor little guy must have had it rough, because he just didn't understand play, at first. Aiden grew up in a wire mesh cage, had bad feet, only 2 teeth and a chewed off ear When he first go to our house all the kids and another puppy were too much for the little guy, he didn't know what to do.

We realized that this poor little guy had either never played or he'd forgotten how. Slowly, he remembered how to wrestle with another dog, chase the kids around and even start a little trouble with the his rescuer. You remember how to play don't you?

Play is an essential component of creativity. The key phrase is "What if?" This playful, childish question comes from curiosity and has led to some of the great discoveries of our time (or any other.) Play is about trying new things, about going with an idea, about riffing. Duh; Play is fun.

The main reason people take up a creative pursuit? Because it is fun, because it gives them satisfaction. Grabbing a guitar and strumming it is cool, so is writing a song or painting a mural.

LAUGHTER: Did you laugh today? I've been through times in my life where the sound of laughter is surprising, when things get so serious that I am surprised and even a little unfamiliar with my own laugh. Have you experienced anything like that?

Creativity comes from joy, from love and it takes a pretty good sense of humor to decide you are an artist at Mid Life. If you doubt that, waltz out to make breakfast in a smock some morning, tell your college kids you are taking Improv, tell your company legal department you are writing a book. Someone will have a laugh, you might as well!

Laughter changes everything, it helps us comprehend the serious, it relieves tension, its fun! Humor is a right brain trait, while your left brain is trying to figure out why the chicken is heading into traffic, your right brain has already seen the irony in the simplicity of, "To get to the other side." Laughter is a pretty good lubricant for creation.

MUSIC: I have a thing with music. We all do, there's something about music that lifts our soul, that takes us away from our current state into a new one. Why do you think it's used in Church? Put some music on for kids and watch what happens, our brains are different on music. Music isn't just notes, music is rhythm, the ebb and flow of life. Music is jiggling your fingers when you walk, it's hearing notes in the wind and in traffic, it's the singing of your babies. Something is different when you have a song in your heart.

In the days before recorded music, the Renaissance artist Leonard da Vinci paid a musician to play while he worked, he also had fragrant flowers and fresh food smells from the kitchen to help in get into creative flow. Music unlocks the Beast's cage.

STORIES: "What kind of life should I lead?" We all face this question everyday and stories help us to make that decision. As famed author and teacher Robert McKee sais, "A good story, well told" is something we all long for. Artists tell stories, no matter what their medium. You have stories to tell, you've ben around a while. When you are running short on inspiration reach into your closet and find a story from your life. Tell us about falling in love, about falling out of love, about something you've overcome, about your failings. A good story, well told is a work of art. So are you.

GRACE: It's been really difficult for me to talk about creation without getting into some kind of religious argument. I hate religious arguments; I find them to be an utter waste of time. So, when I talk about Grace, I'm appropriating a religious term to describe a feeling I don't quite know how else to describe. this feeling of being "One with everything in life." Is a pretty remarkable place to hang out. Grace is creative flow on steroids, it's like being on ecstasy without the glow sticks.

Perhaps the greatest benefit of Releasing my Creative Beast is this particular feeling I call Grace. When I am feeling especially creative and in Grace, inspiration is everywhere, I am surrounded by ideas. Grace is that feeling that you are plugged into your source, that you are not alone, that your ego is under control. I'm not aware of Grace everyday, but when I go looking for it, it always seems to be there.

UNDERSTANDING: Contrast is part of art and being an artist allows you to welcome it. The result? You see both sides of an argument better. How can you write a good story without explaining conflict? You need harmony to make good music, and the artist part of your brain recognizes and works with conflict better than non artists. Spending your day in artistic Grace results in less dogma, less black and white. There is a lot more grey when you accept and recognize that everyone is doing their best, that no one intentionally makes a bad decision. Portraying the grey, the conflict, is a lot of where you find great art.

MAGIC: Magic is what's left. Magic is what happens when your fingers happen to type just the right phrase, it happens when you come up with just the right punch line at Improv, it's when you and your playing partner jam together and create, well, Magic. When you are open to inspiration, when you have settled on your medium, when you are playful and curious, when you feel a little music, the Magic shows up. Magic is what happens when you say, "What if?"

Magic is why you become Creative in the first place, it's the closest you will get to immortality. When you create, when you come up with something no one has ever done before, you are magical. There are only 12 notes, yet there is no end to new musical compositions. When you solve a problem, when see something different than everyone else, when you craft a story that seems to come from beyond, you are magical.

The word enthusiasm comes from the Greek words that mean the God Within. Even the most depressed artist finds some hope, some enthusiasm in creation. That's magic. Whether you believe in Adam or spontaneous combustion, creation contains an element of mystery, something mortals call magic.

Middle Aged Crazy and "When Do I Get to Be Me" are invitations to discover your own magic, to become, if only for a moment, one with creation, one with life. You have an artist inside, a Creative Beast to unleash, why not try it now?

So, what's next what are your action steps? Will you commit to release your Beast, will you make an effort? I'm rooting you do, I'm hoping you've read this far because you have a passion to release, you have stories to tell, you have a song to sing.

Chapter 11 Exercises

1. Give yourself three creative goals for the next twelve months. (That's all, for now.)

2. Now, how much time can you commit per day and how many days a week can you work on your craft?

3. What are you willing to do to improve your ability at your craft (classes etc.)

4. What is your "realistic" art goal, your "Stretch" art goal and your "Big hairy" art goal?

5. Ok, time to apply some creativity. For each of the Creative Attributes I described in this chapter, I'd like you to create something. There are really no rules in this game, simply allow the creative attribute to play in your mind, let it marinate a little and then make something. A story, a picture, a song, it doesn't matter. What do each of these words bring up for you? One can make a different project for each word or any combination of them. The point is, let's get going!

When you are done, please send me a picture or other representation of what you did. I'll figure out a way to get them posted for our community on the Middle Aged Crazy Web Page.

Rick@middleagedcrazy.com

Play

Laughter

Music

Stories

Grace

Understanding

The Creative Beast is alive in you. I hope this little work of love, "When Do I Get to Be Me? " has persuaded you to look at the world a little differently, And, more importantly, I hope it has convinced you to take action! If you aren't ready to dive into a new creative pursuit, I hope you will give it serious thought and read a little more about the concept.
You are a unique and perfect creation yourself, it's time to pay it forward, share your creations with us!
I hope you'll join us at www.middleagedcrazy.com and become a part of our community, you'll find a bunch of grown up kids who have decided it is time to come out and play. So come on out, even if it is just until the streetlights come on!
Rick

ABOUT THE AUTHOR

Rick DiBiasio Released His Creative Beast!

During his 25 years as a successful Wall Street guy, Rick DiBiasio was always a round peg trying to fit into a square hole. This former religious studies and psychology major is still more interested in Wayne Dyer than Warren Buffett. He's more likely to be found playing guitar than playing the market. His financial planning practice, centered around creative and artistic people, has always been about helping people use their assets to find meaning in their life.

When Rick wrote the Affluent Artist, How Creative Could You Be if Money Wasn't an Issue? (Forward by Jack Canfield), he demonstrated his talent to make even the most complex financial issues easy to grasp. Creative people need help welcoming money and abundance into their lives because they ARE different, and it takes a special person to be able to serve as a bridge between the financial and creative worlds. Rick's keynote speeches, break out sessions and full day workshops are entertaining and enlightening experiences that give Right Brainers the power to not only survive, but Thrive in the business community.

Rick's message is to "let your creative side come out and play" while getting a handle on the "money stuff".

"If your job can be outsourced to Asia or automated, you are toast", Rick says, "So what's left? Creativity, that's what! We are at the dawn of a right brain revolution, a new Renaissance. Creatives provide the content that is the air in the basketball. The thing is, you *can* do business from a place of love and abundance."

Middle Aged Crazy, Rick's newest project, enthusiastically examines the other side of the Affluent Artist coin: Successful people who have reached a crossroads in life, who are looking for meaning and want to "release their creative beast." Besides writing a book and a very successful blog, Rick has been busy releasing his inner artist. Since turning 50, Rick has learned to play guitar, embarked on speaking career, made chianti, become a social media expert, learned Italian, taken cooking classes in Italy, learned video editing, taken ballroom dancing, hosted several radio shows. His newest "stretch" is a series of Improv classes.

The Middle Aged Crazy blog is averaging over 1,500 views a week, he has 30,000 Twitter followers and his new Facebook Fan Page already has over 10,000 followers.

Rick is the Father of four and Grandfather of one. When not writing you can usually find him playing guitar for dolphins and manatees on his boat in the Indian River. He lives in Florida.

• ABOUT THE ILLUSTRATOR

She Speaks!

Hi, I'm Betsy. I've been drawing for as long as I can remember. When I was a kid my dad, a computer programmer, used to bring me big stacks of the old tractor-feed computer printout paper to draw on each night, and I would be ready for another stack by the next day.

Creatures like the Creative Beast have crept into my drawings all along – even as I've pursued a career spanning film and video, design, and video games. I published a single-panel cartoon feature, "Brainwaves," for over sixteen years, and I still license cartoons all over the world. I am especially proud to have a cartoon in the Smithsonian Astrophysics Observatory's traveling exhibit on black holes. I also illustrate books for field trips at 826 Valencia in San Francisco.

The arts give people, and especially kids, the power to bring their own voice to the conversation about who they are and how they think. The arts enable us to build and to trust our own inner world, a world that will grow and change as we mature. In a society where we spend way too much time on external things like test scores, college and consuming, we can easily forget to ask who we – and our kids – are. This is what the arts are for.

When we exclude the arts from the education of our young people, we neglect their budding identities and send them the message that "success" is achieved only through external milestones. Hopefully those of us who are reaching midlife and discovering our own creativity, will then reach back to our young people and help them do the same.

Please enjoy this book, and enjoy Releasing Your Creative Beast!

You can learn more about me and my work at
www.betsystreeter.com.

NOTES

Made in the USA
Lexington, KY
27 August 2011